MORE THAN PETTICOATS

Remarkable

OKLAHOMA WOMEN

MORE THAN PETTICOATS

Remarkable
OKLAHOMA WOMEN

Deborah Bouziden

Guilford, Connecticut

To buy books in quantity for corporate use
or incentives, call **(800) 962-0973**
or e-mail **premiums@GlobePequot.com**.

Map by Alena Joy Pearce © Morris Book Publishing, LLC
Project editor: Lauren Brancato
Layout: Justin Marciano

Library of Congress Cataloging-in-Publication Data

Bouziden, Deborah.
More than petticoats. Remarkable Oklahoma women / Deborah Bouziden.
p. cm.
Includes bibliographical references.
ISBN 978-0-7627-6028-2
1. Women—Oklahoma—Biography. 2. Women—Oklahoma—History. 3. Oklahoma—Biography. I. Title. II. Title: Remarkable Oklahoma women.
CT3262.O5B68 2013
920.72—dc23
[B]
2012037200

Printed in the United States of America

10 9 8 7 6 5 4 3 2 1

CONTENTS

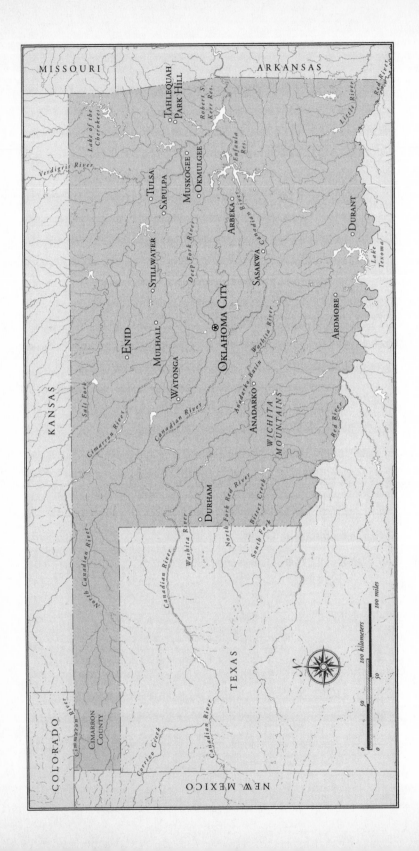

MISSOURI

ARKANSAS

Red River

Red River

TAHLEQUAH ○
PARK HILL ○

Lake of the Cherokees

Robert S. Kerr Res.

Little River

Verdigris River

MUSKOGEE ○
OKMULGEE ○

Eufaula Res.

TULSA ○
SAPULPA ○

DURANT ○

ARBEKA ○

Canadian River

Deep Fork River

SASAKWA ○

Lake Texoma

STILLWATER ○

⊕ OKLAHOMA CITY

ENID ○

MULHALL ○

Salt Fork

WATONGA ○

Washita River

ARDMORE ○

KANSAS

Cimarron River

Canadian River

ANADARKO ○

Anadarko Basin

WICHITA
MOUNTAINS

Red River

North Canadian River

DURHAM ○

Washita River

North Fork Red River

Bitter Creek

South Fork

Canadian River

100 miles

Cimarron River

CIMARRON
COUNTY

TEXAS

100 kilometers

50

50

0

0

COLORADO

Canadian River

Carrizo Creek

NEW MEXICO

N

ACKNOWLEDGMENTS

A book of this type is impossible without the help of others. I enjoyed gathering and sorting through the miles of research material, but without the museum curators and historical researchers pointing me in the right direction, I would have been lost.

First, the T. B. Ferguson Home in Watonga opened its doors, gave me a tour, and allowed me to glimpse what prairie life was like around the turn of the twentieth century. Terri Crawford at the Watonga Library gave me books to read about the governor's wife and the town she called home for years. Robin Willis at the Anadarko Heritage Museum, Rosalie Dawson at the Pioneer Woman Museum in Ponca City, and Carolyn Smith at the Ninety-Nines Museum of Women Pilots in Oklahoma City took the time to pull reference material for me and discuss the lives of the ladies whose backgrounds and histories were in their care. Dennis Miles at Southeastern Oklahoma State University in Durant helped me gain access to materials I wouldn't and couldn't have found on my own.

Next is Martha Berry, who spent hours of her time answering my e-mails and talking to me on the phone about her great aunt, Rachel Caroline Eaton. It was refreshing to hear family stories and know there are those out there who are just as passionate about the past as they are about the future. I agree with her about history and aspects of the Cherokee Nation.

Finally, I'd like to offer a special thanks to the staff at the Oklahoma History Center in Oklahoma City. Jennifer Day made my research easier by showing me how to access the center's computer system at home and pulled countless archive files for me. Dr. Debra Spindle, Steve Hawkins, and Bernie DeWitt helped me look for information in the stacks, pulled books for me behind the desk, fixed the copier more times than I can remember, let me in and out of the center's secured area more than they'd like to remember, and reminded me I did occasionally need to take a break. Thanks, guys, for keeping it real.

> *We cannot dedicate, we cannot consecrate, we cannot hallow this ground. The brave [wo]men, living and dead, who struggled here, have consecrated it, far above our poor power to add or detract.*
>
> *The world will little note, nor long remember what we say here, but it can never forget what they did here.*

—ABRAHAM LINCOLN, GETTYSBURG ADDRESS

INTRODUCTION

When I first started this book, I knew it would be an incredible journey. I have always loved history, and knowing I would be discovering and writing about women who had made a difference in my home state excited and intrigued me.

I have been asked how I chose these particular twelve women. It was no easy task. I started by asking friends and fellow Oklahomans to give me the names of women who had impressed them in Oklahoma history. The list grew to over one hundred names. I then narrowed the list to twenty-five according to the region of Oklahoma they called home. From there, I decided to write small sketches of 100 to 150 words on each and look at each of their contributions. After looking at their lives, I narrowed the list down to the twelve showcased here because something about their lives spoke to me: the things they did against the odds, the hurdles they cleared, and the obstacles they overcame by their own pluck and courage. Not all of their lives ended gloriously. While these women shared a commitment to help others, in the end many died alone and penniless. Yet, their stories remain.

To understand what they did, I knew I had to understand where they came from, their families, their early years, and not only their good sides but their dark sides as well. I had to understand what drove them, what their hopes, dreams, and goals were.

Another challenge was to condense these women's multifaceted lives to the few pages allotted for each entry. Citing only their grand achievements would leave an incomplete picture, ignoring difficulties and unrealized potential. For example, deaths of loved ones made them stronger but at the same time also took something away from them. Many of their lives could have been easier and their contributions greater had not political wheels been turning, threatening and then destroying many of their hopes and dreams.

While striving to give the most complete picture possible, I was guided by three goals: I wanted readers to read about these women and want to learn more about them. I wanted readers to be inspired and motivated by their lives. And finally, I wanted readers to remember them.

If people read this book, and a couple weeks or months later, they talk about one of the women around the water cooler at work, think about a certain woman and decide they can reach for their dreams like one of my subjects did, or become motivated to make a change in their community from the example set in one of these women's lives, then I have accomplished my goals.

As I said, this book has not been easy. My biggest fear is that I will not have done these women justice. As time marches on, what these women accomplished in the past has made all of our lives better. Their contribution may have been small or it may have been large, but in the end the biggest accomplishment is that they did things their way and to the best of their abilities. Their lives should be celebrated not only on the pages of this book, but in the lives of generations to come.

Of course there are many more Oklahoma women worthy of being called "remarkable" than this set of twelve. Of special note are Winonah Leah Monroney, Kathryn Nedry Van Leuven, and Edith Rhoda Force Kassing. These and a few others would be in these pages if enough had been written about them. Researchers are continuing to gather material on these outstanding Oklahomans, and I hope that their stories can someday soon be told as well.

In the meantime, I hope you will read about the women portrayed here, learn from their experiences, be motivated by their accomplishments, and be inspired by their courage.

I am.

CATHERINE "KATE" ANN BARNARD

(1875–1930)

CHILD ADVOCATE AND VOICE
FOR THE POOR

" I want to feel that the world is better because I have lived in it," Kate wrote in an article for *Sturm's Oklahoma Magazine* on the eve of the first Oklahoma Legislature's meeting. "I am especially interested in that class of legislation that will best protect the tiniest and frailest bit of humanity that is entrusted to our care. I am especially interested in child-life, because our fathers represent the past, we the present, and the children represent the future. I am interested in the passage of laws that will make it possible for the poorest child to receive an education—not only of letters and of books, but of lands."

Diminutive Catherine Ann Barnard, whom everyone from the homeless to governors called Kate, had three goals: to help the down-trodden, enrich children's lives, and give hope to those living in despair. She knew the loneliness of being motherless, yet managed to fill that emptiness with outstanding achievements that nurtured her own spirit and certainly nurtured others She believed in the goodness of people. Even when politicians, newspapers, and friends turned on her for doing what she thought was right and good for the state, she pressed on. When she became so ill she couldn't get out of bed, she still pressed on. Not for herself, but for others.

Catherine Ann Barnard was born in Alexandria, Nebraska, on May 23, 1875, to John Barnard and Rachel Shiell Mason. Her father had come

Catherine Ann Barnard Courtesy of the Research Division of the Oklahoma Historical Society, Oklahoma City

to America from Ireland when he was eight months old. He had a strong work ethic, which he instilled in Kate, and worked as a civil engineer, lawyer, surveyor, and railroad worker. Kate's mother, Rachel, had been married before she met John and had two sons. The couple married in 1873 in Geneva, Nebraska.

In January 1877, when Kate was just over a year and a half old, her mother and week-old brother died. Even though Kate wasn't old enough to know what was happening, this event would shape the rest of her life.

Soon after, her father sent the three children to live with his wife's parents while he left town to seek work. As he traveled from one position to another, Kate went from relative to relative. She seldom saw her father, but she idolized him. "My love for my father and a desire to help the poor became the two great dominant factors of my life. His example provided the moral strength behind every sacrifice for principle, every struggle for liberty, and every achievement recorded," she said later in life. He remained her constant. Her maternal grandmother decided she would raise Kate's two stepbrothers, but not her, so they were never a part of Kate's life.

In 1881, four-year-old Kate moved back in with her father and his new wife, Anna Teresa Rose. They settled in Kensington, Kansas. Kate was excited about her new life and time as a family, but two years into the marriage, Anna divorced Kate's father, leaving her motherless again. The couple had a son together, but Kate never knew her baby brother either.

This time, John took Kate with him in his search for work. The pair stayed with strangers and was never in one place long enough for Kate to get along in school or make friends. When Kate was thirteen, her father suffered financial setbacks that left them penniless, and they almost starved in their struggle to survive. A year later, Kate's father left her again and headed to the Oklahoma Territory, where he participated in the Land Run of 1889. After he had built a two-room dwelling, he sent for Kate. Their first stake was in a little town to the east of Oklahoma City called Newalla. Kate lived on the property by herself while her father worked in Oklahoma City as an attorney. It was a lonely time for Kate, and on days she despaired. However, when she turned eighteen, she moved to Oklahoma City at 209 West Reno, where her father had purchased property and built them a small house.

After she settled in with her father, her next order of business was to finish her schooling, which she did at St. Joseph's Parochial School. Although she couldn't afford to go to college, Kate was smart enough to pass the teacher's test and get her certificate from the Oklahoma State Board of Education. Kate's teaching career was destined to be a short one. In fact she had decided long ago on those lonely nights in Newalla what she wanted to do with her life: She wanted to help alleviate the suffering of the unfortunate. Now she became more committed, as she saw daily the sufferings of the poor in the area where she and her father lived, which was the red light district, a dilapidated Oklahoma City slum. She especially grieved for the children, and set her goal to become "a voice for those who suffered in the gutter of humanity."

There didn't seem to be enough happening with Kate's teaching to keep her energy bridled, and it certainly wasn't helping her reach her goals. So she decided to study stenography and gain secretarial skills so she could get a more challenging job. She found it when she took on a job as a stenographer and clerk in Guthrie, Oklahoma, for the Republican minority in the territorial legislature. It was here that she got a small glimpse of what politics was all about.

After working for several months in the legislature, an opportunity arose that she couldn't pass up. She competed with 498 other participants to represent Oklahoma at the World's Fair in St. Louis, Missouri. She was chosen, and in 1904, at the age of twenty-nine, went to St. Louis as secretary and hostess of the Oklahoma Territory exhibit. While there, she spoke to exhibition leaders, did interviews, and talked about

Oklahoma to visitors in general. She loved Oklahoma and wanted others to see the state in a favorable light. She also was able to attend meetings of humanitarian organizations where she heard not only about the plight of the poor, but also about reforms being made to help them. She wrote impassioned letters about what she was learning to the *Daily Oklahoman*. She also took her information to a local St. Louis paper. The editor at that paper assigned a reporter to Kate, and the pair went to every slum in the city. Kate got a view of life she couldn't have imagined existed.

After the World's Fair the *Daily Oklahoman* paid for her to attend Graham Taylor's Chicago School of Civics and Philanthropy so that she could write a series of articles. While she was *seeing* the problem, she traveled to Chicago and Denver to find *answers* to it.

She had made a strong ally in the *Daily Oklahoman* and became known and respected by its readership. So when she returned to Oklahoma, and wrote articles asking those who had an abundance to give to the less fortunate, or when she ran an advertisement asking for food and clothing, the community responded generously.

While she continued this humanitarian work, she also briefly held a job as stenographer for a city attorney, but was fired because she wouldn't work on Sunday and seemed more interested in the plights of the poor than her job. That only spurred her on. In December 1905, she took over and reorganized the United Provident Association. From 1905 to 1907 the group served over two thousand families in need. She joined labor organizations, fought for higher wages, and became a voice for those she felt would not only advance her causes but also help those in need.

Kate took her mission statewide. She traveled and made forty-four speeches before the November 1906 election. With statehood and a new state constitution on the way, she wanted to make sure that the reforms she championed would be guaranteed in the new constitution and that Oklahoma would become an example for other states. She campaigned for those who agreed with her. And while Kate's ideas were considered progressive and new to most Oklahomans, people listened to her.

Most important, the delegates listened to her, and when she was allowed to address the constitutional convention, she emphasized three proposals for the new constitution. First was a ban on child labor; second, a proposal for compulsory education; and third, a plan to create an office of Commissioner of Charities and Corrections. Because of Kate's immense popularity, lawmakers took notice of her suggestions. Oklahoma, in fact, became the first state to have a child labor plank included in its constitution. In the end, Kate got everything she asked for. The delegates had adopted a child labor ban, which determined the age at which a child could work and how many hours per day, set up a plan of education for children, required children ages 8 to 16 to attend school, and created the office of Commissioner of Charities and Corrections. This office would oversee charitable organizations and the state's prison system.

Kate was elated, especially so when she was chosen to run for the new office of Commissioner of Charities and Corrections. She saw it as an opportunity to safeguard newly won reforms and to bring further reforms to her new state. When the dust settled and the votes were counted on September 17, 1907, Kate had won by a landslide. She was not only the top vote-getter in Oklahoma's first election, but the only woman elected to a state office when women did not even have the right to vote yet.

After the election, lawmakers and state officers set to work implementing the new constitution. Within their ranks now, Kate began the job of overseeing 325 jails, poorhouses, orphanages, rescue homes, and institutions for the care of children, the blind, deaf, and insane on a local, city, and statewide level.

At first, her department received enough money to do the job for which it was commissioned. But Kate had made enemies, and one of the biggest was "Alfalfa" Bill Murray. He fought her on her reforms because he didn't feel they were needed, but mostly because she was a woman. She was successful—some say instrumental—in one of his election bid losses, and he would be back with more venom than Kate could handle.

While she was happy in her legislative success, her father's death on May 5, 1909, overshadowed that contentment. "He was the one being for whom I hoped to share my ambitions and my successes. It was to bring credit on his name that I strove so hard," she said after his death. Even though, his death hit her hard mentally and physically, it did leave her financially well off.

During her two terms in office, she was instrumental in getting children out of mines, harmful factories, and sweatshops, and into schools. She helped reform penal housing and had hundreds of prisoners held in Kansas prisons returned to Oklahoma. She helped institute eight-hour workdays and set limitations on where and when children could work when they were not in school. Kate also championed children convicted of crimes by reforming the juvenile justice system.

Her greatest fight and perhaps the one that brought about her demise was when she began reforms to recover and return Indian lands and monies to orphaned Indian children. When Indian lands were opened to white settlers, the government claimed the right to govern the Indians' finances as well. The government gave the Indians, children and adults alike, a certain amount of money for the land whites were now settling. In the case of Indian orphans, a guardian was placed in charge of them and their monies.

The whole business came to Kate's attention when some citizens in the eastern part of the state reported seeing fairies in the woods. Upon investigating, Kate discovered the "fairies" were three orphaned Indian children, starving, wearing rags, and living among the trees. Upon further inquiry, she found that the guardian was living off the children's allotment and not taking care of their welfare. Not only that, but she discovered this wasn't the only case. With the help of a newly hired attorney, her office began exposing cases like these as well as other types of corruption, exposing not only well-to-do Oklahoma citizens, but politicians as well.

The more she fought for reform and legislation, the more the politicians fought back. The more corruption she found and the harder she fought, the more her office was whittled down, until only Kate and one stenographer were left. She informed one of her supporters that she would not campaign for re-election of a third term. Instead, she would devote the rest of her time and energy on Indian issues and securing the protection of Indian property rights.

By 1914 Kate had been fighting an illness she couldn't recover from. She had contracted a severe form of type one herpes simplex virus that undermined her health. As her political influence was fading because of her health, Bill Murray launched a vicious campaign against her Indian rights work. It was a regrettably successful venture, resulting in the press's dissemination of false information about not only her personally, but her work. On January 12, 1915, she acknowledged defeat, packed up her belongings, and moved out of the office of Charities and Corrections. In the seven years she served, she had found her place and identity, but now it was time to move on.

Kate left the state, traveling to Colorado and Hot Springs, Arkansas, in an attempt to recover her health. She was so removed now from the centers of Oklahoma power that people began hearing rumors that she was dead. Yet from her sick bed she still wrote letters to people she thought could further the Indian cause and assist in helping the poor. By now, though, politicians considered her a joke. The bill that had been drafted at her request in regard to the Indian issue was not adopted. She realized all hope of ever getting it through the state legislature was lost.

At the end of October 1915, she had recuperated enough to go on a speaking tour in the east. She thought if Oklahoma wouldn't tackle the

Indian issue, the federal government might, if she could generate enough interest. It was not to be. Totally exhausted after she could get no support, she had a relapse. Her heart was broken, and she gave up.

"I love my state, my father is buried in its soil. I love every tree and flower and I could scream my agony as I am compelled to pen these lines to you. But God knows there is no justice for Indians in Oklahoma. The only hope lies in Washington," Kate wrote in a letter to her friend and supporter, Walter L. Fisher, Illinois Republican and secretary of the interior under President Taft. "Truly, I don't know why I was born. This battle is too much for me. It would kill a strong man."

Depressed and still battling her incurable illness, she closed the door on public life in 1916 and left Oklahoma City. She made a new home in Denver, but traveled frequently in the next ten years in an effort to find a cure or some relief from her disease, which was worsening. Her stress-induced herpes blisters, once confined to her mouth, were now breaking out all over her body.

She returned to Oklahoma City in 1926, but she lived as a recluse, seldom venturing from her room at the Egbert Hotel. Though isolated, she was still focused on improving the lives of others, this time working on a book about women and politics. At night, guests complained about the click of her typewriter. By 1929 both her physical and mental health had rapidly deteriorated. She became paranoid, imagining conspiracies threatening her and the Department of Charities and Corrections.

In February 1930 on a cold Sunday afternoon, a hotel maid found Kate in the bathtub of her living quarters. She was dead. The coroner pronounced her cause of death as heart failure. Her body was removed to the coroner's office and her relatives were notified. They refused any involvement in funeral arrangements. Finally, a friend stepped in and took care of the service. Fourteen hundred people showed up at her service, which was held at St. Joseph's Catholic Church. Former governors were honorary pall bearers and the flag at the Capitol was flown at half-mast in her honor. The funeral procession traveled to Fairlawn Cemetery where Kate was laid to rest beside her father.

Kate reached the pinnacle of popularity and success in her short political career helping the unfortunate. She was truly "Oklahoma's Angel." Through her reform ideas and a connection with a new state legislature, she saw what Oklahoma could be and she wanted the best for "her" state. She would be proud of the work that has been accomplished in the name of reform over the last decades, but she also would know there is a lot more work to be done as there always is in any civilized society.

ALICE BROWN DAVIS

(1852–1935)

CHIEF OF THE SEMINOLE

"I wish to declare that Mrs. Davis does not attain this high honor through her relationship to the former chief," Major Victor M. Locke Jr., Superintendent of the Five Civilized Tribes, said in 1922 at the ceremony to swear in Alice Brown Davis as Chieftess of the Seminole. "She is a woman of distinction in her own right, and has demonstrated time and time again, by a life of usefulness and hard work, such qualifications as may be required for the attainment of the highest honors authorized in the political schemes of government peculiar to Indian Tribes."

Without this appointment, Alice Brown Davis would probably have gone down in history as Chief John Franklin Brown's little sister and into obscurity. Hers was a hard and difficult life.

She knew about sacrifice. She lived in a time of tremendous change, not only in the nation, but specifically in Oklahoma. She saw and felt the consequences of war, outbreaks of diseases that killed friends and family members, buffalo migrations, a period of lawlessness, Indian Territory being opened for white settlement, the struggle for statehood and then its fruition, the oil boom, the women's rights struggle, and Oklahoma's transition from a frontier land to a modern society.

More importantly for Alice, whose mother was Seminole, she also experienced the effect of US government policies affecting the Seminoles before, during, and after not only the Civil War, but World War I. Throughout these tumultuous times, her service was dedicated to the Seminole, and like her brother, she sought their best interest at every juncture. This wasn't always easy, but she faced adversities with dignity, determination, and courage.

Alice Brown Davis Courtesy of the Research Division of the Oklahoma Historical Society, Oklahoma City

Alice and a twin sister, Zora, were born on the morning of September 10, 1852, at Parkhill, Indian Territory, five miles southeast of Tahlequah, the capital of the Cherokee Nation. Unfortunately, her sister died later that day.

Her parents were John Frippo Brown and Lucy Redbeard. They both had traveled west on the Trail of Tears. John Frippo Brown, a Scotsman, was a physician who had been commissioned to travel with and take care of the soldiers as they moved the Seminoles to their new home in Indian Territory. Lucy Redbeard, a member of the Tiger Clan, a royal clan of the Seminole nation, also known as Kunu Hvt'ke, or White Skunk, was one of the survivors of the Trail. It was after both their arrivals in Park Hill that they met, fell in love, and determined to get married. He was twenty-three years older than Lucy, who was just nineteen. Her clan had provided chiefs for the Seminole tribe since its beginnings, and her romantic involvement with an outsider was not looked on favorably. The couple touted convention, however, and married anyway.

Even though the tribe did not take kindly to the union, the couple was soon forgiven and settled near current-day Konawa, Oklahoma, in the southwest corner of Seminole County. The couple had eight children. Their son John Franklin Brown, Alice's oldest brother, would become Chief of the Seminoles some years after he served in the Civil War.

Alice's father, Dr. John Brown, established a private medical practice after he and Lucy married, but his practice in Konawa couldn't always generate enough income to keep his family clothed and fed. So he decided to take commissioned jobs with the army. These took their own toll on the family. Brown would have to travel distances and in some cases be gone from home for long periods of time. Lucy was left to take care of the children herself. He finally decided the sacrifice of being away from his family was too great and returned to his local practice.

When the Civil War broke out, Alice's father moved his family to Fort Gibson. John Franklin Brown, Alice's brother, joined the Seminole chief, John Jumper, in fighting for the Confederates. Doctor Brown remained neutral while ordered to tend to wounded soldiers coming into the fort. Many were the days that wagons brought in dead and dying Confederate and Union soldiers. He looked through each one wondering if his eldest son was among them.

After the war ended, the family moved to Greenhead Prairie, in present day Pottawatomie County. This was not a happy time in Seminole history. During the war, half of the Seminoles fought for the Confederacy and half for the Union. When the Union won, the government punished *all* the Seminoles by dividing their original land allotment in half. While bad for the Seminoles, it was a stroke of luck for Alice's father and his family. Dr. Brown was able to acquire the Seminole Agency building taken away from the Seminoles as part of their punishment.

During their childhood, Alice and her siblings' educations were not ignored. A graduate of the University of Edinburgh himself, their father, who kept a well-used library, wanted his children to be educated as well.

Alice, along with her siblings, attended both Cherokee and Seminole schools, but Alice also learned a great deal by spending time with her beloved father. At night she would watch him as he wrote down cures and concoctions for specific ailments. She loved to watch the quill pen fly across the paper. She would ask questions about what he was writing, and he would share with her his regimes and potions to help restore health to his patients. His goal was to create several volumes of remedies that had worked for his patients to pass on to other physicians. At age fourteen Alice was going with him on his neighborhood rounds, carrying his supplies and helping him care for the sick.

During the time she spent with her father, she also learned about where he was born and where he grew up. She listened closely as her father told stories of far-off Scotland and what might as well have been as far away, Charleston, South Carolina. Her father's descriptions made her want to visit these places, but she doubted she ever would. Still benefiting from her father's influence, Alice also learned a great deal from pouring over the books in his library. There she discovered Dickens, Shakespeare, and other classical writers, many of whom she could quote and discuss at length. Alice also read the Bible, another mainstay in the Brown family home. In fact, from an early age she began reading one chapter a day, a practice that comforted her for the rest of her life.

In 1867, when Alice was fifteen, a cholera epidemic broke out and swept through the Seminole Nation. For weeks, Alice and her father rode out day after day, trying to help those who were afflicted. Even though he was exhausted, Dr. Brown kept going. His wife, Lucy, and Alice tried to convince him to rest, but he wouldn't. He mounted his horse one morning, but slipped out of the saddle before they left their property. Alice got him back inside the house, but he passed away during the night. He was simply worn out.

Three months later, Alice's mother, Lucy, at the age of forty-seven, collapsed at home. Alice and her sister Sukey tried to get their mother to the government doctor in Wewoka, the new Seminole capital, but they were too late.

Her eldest brother, John, head of the family since their father's death, took charge and moved his siblings back to Seminole County. Alice and her brothers and sisters continued their education under his watchful eye. After her parents died, Alice spent twelve months studying at a Presbyterian boarding school north of Wewoka while her brother opened a trading post at Sasakwa, in the middle of a large prairie located in the southeast part of the Seminole Nation.

When she returned home, she lived with her brother, his wife, their children, and her six other siblings in her brother's house at Sasakwa. Since she was an educated woman, she taught school for the girls in their small town and acted as clerk for her brother's trading post. A younger brother, Jackson Brown, was accountant for the business. It was at this trading post that Alice met her future husband, George Rollin Davis.

He sauntered through the door looking for products he could buy for his employer, J. E. Jones, a trader in Okmulgee. He made arrangements to buy pecans and animal furs at a wholesale rate from Alice's brother. This would put him in the trading post over and over again. Alice eventually became as smitten with George as he was with her, and on January 20, 1874, the couple was married by the Creek principal chief and pastor of the Indian Methodist Church, Reverend Sam Chocote.

The couple made their home in Okmulgee. George continued working for Jones right after the couple was married, but eventually went to work for F. E. Severs and the Moore family. These jobs were an education for him. He learned how to run a trading post, raise cattle, and tend farm and ranch land. The couple also started a family. In October of 1874, Alice gave birth to their first child, a daughter whom they named Katie Jane. She only lived three months. From 1876 to 1879, Alice had three more children, George Lytle, Clara Estelle, and Jesse Edwin.

In 1882, the couple decided they wanted some land, a large acreage to start a cattle ranch, raise their family, and start a business of their own, a trading post. They would set up their store and make goods available to the Creek Indians. They settled on a piece of property twenty miles north of Wewoka, along the North Canadian River.

Alice and Roll were excited with their choice of property. They talked about all they needed, set pencil to paper, and it wasn't long until their dream started to become a reality. They quickly decided on a name for their ranch. It would forever be known as the Bar X Bar. The location for the trading post and proposed post office would be called Arbeka.

In 1885, Alice's brother, John Franklin Brown, at the age of forty-two became Chief of the Seminoles. While he was busy dealing with policies the white men were throwing at the Seminoles and building boarding schools like Mekusukey and Emahaka, his sister and her husband were making a go of it at Arbeka. In the mid-1890s, their seven thousand head of cattle roamed the open range, watched, herded, and protected by twenty cowboys, two of whom were Alice and Roll's eldest sons. The Trading Post was doing well with a steady stream of business.

Alice had it all. She had her big white house with a picket fence, servants, and ten children. John Frippo Davis, her youngest, had just turned one, and her oldest, George Lytle Davis, was eighteen and now married. Alice was forty-two. She had taught her children manners, insisted on orderliness in her home, and had strictly disciplined her brood. She was proud of the things she and Roll had accomplished.

She enjoyed an easy routine: She would get up early; make her feather bed, which the children were not allowed to touch, much less get on; read her Bible; and make sure a big pot of chicken and rice soup was on the stove for any visitors who might stop by. And stop by they did. Creeks, Seminoles, and even whites stopped by to talk to Alice and ask for advice about problems in their lives, be it personal or business. She could communicate in their tongue, would listen, and because a lot of their worries were the same as hers, she could offer good suggestions.

Alice was glad to have extra help at the ranch. Having a cook was especially helpful, and her eldest son's wife, Julia, had a sister, Victoria Banash, who filled the job nicely. In February 1895, Alice gave birth to her eleventh child, Andrew Jackson Davis. By April, Alice felt like there was something amiss in her home. She couldn't quite pin it down until she started noticing Victoria was acting extremely strange.

Alice's world was shattered when she discovered Roll, her husband, had been having an affair with the cook, and that Victoria was pregnant with his child. She confronted the pair. Roll packed his clothes, loaded up a buggy, and left Arbeka with Victoria. Their son was born that December.

Alice went to her brother, John Franklin, for advice. He suggested they spread the rumor that George went out gambling, as was rumored he did anyway, drank too much, was robbed, and died. Alice eventually did get a divorce, but she took her time. George and Victoria were finally able to and did get married on December 27, 1897.

The demise of her marriage left Alice alone with the ranch, trading post, and her children, the youngest of whom was just a small child. It also left Alice with what would become a life of heartaches and hardships. It was the end of the easy era of her life and the beginning of a hard one.

In 1899, Alice could see her world changing. With all her girls away at boarding school, only four of her children remained at the ranch. The government had decided to number all the Indians. Supposedly in an attempt to give each Indian a plot of land, they had surveyed Indian Territory, putting markers up designating which land belonged to each tribe and white man, and were requiring all ranchers to fence their property, ending free range. Alice didn't know how the Bar X Bar would survive. Her cattle had roamed the free range since the ranch started.

When November came, Alice was hit by another personal blow. Her firstborn, George Lytle, who was her right-hand man on the ranch, left one morning to check on some cattle. Later that evening she received word he had been hanged by some overzealous lawmen for horse rustling.

With her husband and son gone, she would never be able to fence the family land to keep their cattle in. She could see how things were changing and not for the better, and that she was helpless to do anything about it. Depression and sadness nearly overwhelmed her when she heard that her six-month-old grandson died.

However, Alice knew she had to go on. The Dawes Commission offered her a job as interpreter for the courts. With money in short supply, she took the opportunity. She was well equipped for the job, and it exposed her to other opportunities, like travel.

In 1903, she traveled to Mexico with Chief Hulputta Micco. He had replaced her brother as chief when John Franklin lost the election of 1902, 340 votes to 173. Their mission to Mexico was to lay claim to some property the Seminoles had been promised in 1849. Alice was to be interpreter, but the trip came to naught. The Seminoles tried to negotiate something with Mexico for several years thereafter, but they never did get the land.

Alice did get a break the following year when several members of her family, including brothers and sisters, got to attend the St. Louis World's Fair for a few weeks. Alice had sold some of the family's belongings to get money for the trip for her and her two youngest children. It was also around this time that she had to give up Arbeka and move back in with her brother in Sasakwa. Financially, she couldn't keep the ranch and trading post running. She was barely surviving.

Chief Micco passed away in 1905, and her brother once again became chief. It wasn't a job he sought as he was doing fine serving as minister of the Spring Baptist Church and building his businesses. Alice watched and listened as her brother paced the floor and contemplated how to handle his tribe's relationship with the government. They continued to lie and steal from his people, and basically he was powerless to do anything about it. The biggest contention was the land they continued to take from them.

A year after he took office, he appointed Alice principal of Emahaka, the girl's boarding school. Alice was good in her role, so when the government stepped in and wanted to change the way students were educated here, she was naturally upset. Her girls had attended the school here and left with a fine education. Besides, under Alice's administration, attendance was up by 112 students. But the government had decided to put a new principal in. Alice fought the change at first, but after a while her brother convinced her it was useless to fight Washington. She gave up her position, but would never forget what the government had done.

After Oklahoma became a state, Alice continued to worry about money problems. Her salary as an interpreter was meager, and she used it up quickly continually bailing her two youngest sons out of trouble and paying for her daughters' educations back east. But a couple of trips distracted her in the following years. On two separate occasions, she decided to travel with her brother Jackson to Florida on missionary trips. They spoke to Seminoles who didn't make the migration west. They shared the gospel and encouraged them to read the Bible and contemplate the peace its words could bring.

Alice went back to Mexico in 1910. The Seminole hopes were that the Mexican government would have a change of heart with a change of government, but it wasn't to be. She continued to struggle and saw few rewards for her efforts. Her daughters got married. Her youngest sons married, but as they sought their fortunes in other places than Oklahoma, they continued to write and ask for money. Besides her interpreting, Alice raised chickens and sold their eggs for what she could get for them. She worked hard to get ahead financially.

At age sixty-eight, Alice once again had reason to reflect on her life. Cataracts began to affect her eyesight. Her eldest brother, John Franklin, died at his home on October 21, 1919, and her ex-husband died at her daughter Maude's home in December.

She did not attend George's funeral even though her children requested she do so. Alice was tired and she didn't see the need to travel to the funeral of someone who had left her years ago.

Alice watched the changes that had come to her people at the hands of the Washington government. While they had told her people that the changes were in their best interest, Alice never saw any good. Like her brother, she was helpless to stop the changes they were making. If her people didn't agree with the changes being made, the government changed the rules and simply took what they wanted regardless of what the Indians wanted.

In 1921, some of what the government had done to the Indians came to light. The government had moved so quickly in some instances that certain land deeds that needed to be signed by the Indian chiefs were overlooked. This presented a problem as the Seminoles had no chief since John Franklin Brown had died. President Warren G. Harding appointed Alice as Seminole Chief, but instead of cowing to the Washington establishment and doing what the government wanted done quickly, Alice took her time, read each document, and then decided if it was worth her signature. One document she refused to sign. It concerned the Emahaka Mission Academy, the boarding school where Alice had been principal all those many years ago. The government was selling it right out from under the Seminoles. Alice refused to sign that document and left with the papers.

Alice, for all intents and purposes, served only a month as chief, but made a big impact. The Bureau of Indian Affairs realized they couldn't bend her to do their will and couldn't use her as a tool to get what they wanted when they wanted it. When she continued to stand strong against the government's exploitation of Emahaka, they basically fired her and appointed another chief. He too refused to sign on the grounds that Chief Davis wouldn't sign it, so neither would he.

When the Great Depression of 1929 hit, the government decided it had bigger things to worry about than land in former Indian Territory. Alice continued to keep a watchful eye on what was happening with her family, the government, and her people. As the oil boom hit, she watched as the white man moved in, took land, and became rich at the expense of Indians. She watched other Indian tribes become wealthy as well, while the Seminoles didn't benefit. She also watched as the government doled out money at the rate they felt was needed to the Indians.

On November 12, 1930, she had the opportunity to tell her side of the story to an Indian Affairs subcommittee sent to Oklahoma by the US Senate. She testified about officials stealing land, money, about the lack of schools and hospitals for the Seminoles, and the lack of confidence the Seminoles felt for the government because of all the lies they had told them.

"It would not take one day," she told the committee, "but one month to enumerate all the grievances."

In March 1932, Alice's daughter Maude became ill and died. This was another reminder to her of how fragile life was. Alice had to be careful when she remembered the past, what had come, and what now was gone.

Alice's eyes continued to be a problem, and her health gradually began to slip away, but she lived comfortably in her little white house in Wewoka. Friends came by frequently, and she continued to welcome them into her home, giving them advice when they asked for it and listening to their troubles. Having been to the hospital in Oklahoma City, she begged her daughter to take her home to Wewoka. Irene did take her home, but in June her doctor decided she needed to be admitted again, this time to the Wewoka hospital. Like her father, Alice's heart wore out. Her grandson, Tob, came to pray with her every day at the hospital.

"I am ready, Tob," she told him one day. "The Maker has forgiven my sins. I am prepared to go to Jesus."

Alice Brown Davis passed away peacefully at the Wewoka hospital on Friday, June 21, 1935. She left behind six daughters, two sons, and many grandchildren. She was true to the end to her people, the Seminoles, doing her best to help them in any way she possibly could.

In 1930, she was inducted in to the Oklahoma Hall of Fame, and in 1961 she was honored in the American Indian Hall of Fame. The University of Oklahoma named the Davis House for her in 1950. In 1964, a bronze bust of her was unveiled at the New York World's Fair. It is currently located at the American Indian Hall of Fame in Anadarko, Oklahoma.

Her life was one of hardship and resilience, but through it all she was true to her beliefs and herself. As first female chief of the Seminoles, she was determined to do what was right for her people and she did, standing firm in her belief of fairness and right.

ANGIE DEBO

(1890–1988)

CHRONICLER OF AMERICAN INDIANS

Angie Debo may not have been born in Oklahoma, but her spirit is more Oklahoman than a lot of those who were. Before Oklahoma became a state, it was Indian Territory, a place where the US government relocated Indians of the east. Debo spent her adult life learning about the different Indian groups moved to Oklahoma, the injustices done to them, their renewed spirits, their governments, their customs, and their ways of life. She wrote about all she learned, hoping to educate others about their plight and hopefully make changes on their behalf. She also wrote stories about the pioneering spirit and the men and women who came to Indian Territory to settle it. Debo knew what it was like to be a pioneer. She was one herself.

While early in her career she was passed over for jobs, faced starvation, and was harshly criticized for her work, today her name is held in high esteem and she is known as "Oklahoma's greatest historian." Debo has been honored many times over for the work she did to record Oklahoma's history—good, bad, and ugly.

Angie Elbertha Debo was born in Beattie, Kansas, on January 30, 1890, to Edward and Lina Debo. Once in school, she acquired a love of reading from an early teacher, Miss Gleason, who also figured in another kind of education for young Debo. When Miss Gleason came under fire for failing one of her students, the school board and members of the community accused her of favoritism to Catholic children over Protestant. Debo protested to her parents, "That wasn't true what they said about Mrs. Gleason that she was only good to Catholic children. She let me read to her and I'm not a Catholic." This incident settled into Debo's heart and character. She pledged never to let bigotry enter into anything she did in her life.

Her parents owned a farm in Kansas, but a severe drought, declining crop prices, and a depression soon had them looking for other opportunities. Upon hearing about the positive economic potential of the land known as Indian Territory, they sold out and decided to give the Territory a try. So at age nine, Debo, her parents, and her younger brother, Edwin, boarded a covered wagon and set out for Oklahoma. Their journey ended on November 8, 1899, when they reached the little community of Marshall, in an area that had opened in the land run of April 1899. The dwelling they moved into was little more than a shack, but Angie's father and brother went to work expanding it into a three-room house, while Debo helped her mother with the household chores. Debo would always be extremely close to her family, and the values they taught her—hard work, honesty, and resilience—would hold her in good stead all her life.

Compared to Kansas, Oklahoma offered so much more to see and do, and Angie recorded her new adventures in the pages of her diary, which she'd begun early on. She was a bright little girl, on the lookout for Indians as her Oklahoma adventure began in the wagon lumbering over the grassy plains. She knew Indians should be in Oklahoma, but the only people Angie saw were other settlers and cowboys. This didn't dampen her spirits.

When school started, she loved it. She and her brother made the daily two-mile trek to Rosenberg School, a one-room frame building. Debo admired her first Oklahoma teacher, Stella Noble. In class, they studied a variety of subjects—arithmetic, grammar, and history, to name a few. In history, she learned not only about the Indians, but about the movement of the Indians into Indian Territory and how the Cherokee, Chickasaw, Creek, Choctaw, and Seminole became known as the Five Civilized Tribes. It wasn't long until Angie declared when she grew up she wanted to be "an old maid and teach school."

Angie Debo Courtesy of the Angie Debo Papers, collection 1988–013, Special Collections and University Archives, Oklahoma State University, Stillwater.

Debo finished eighth grade at the age of twelve. Marshall didn't have a school beyond eighth grade, so she waited until she was sixteen, got her teaching certificate, and began teaching school herself. She taught in Logan and Garfield Counties, traveling from farmhouse to farmhouse. While she enjoyed making her salary of thirty-three dollars a month, she quickly tired of the traveling.

In 1910, Marshall got a new high school, and at the age of twenty-three, three years later, Debo, along with eight other students, received her diploma. While a drought and more hard times came upon the Debo family, Angie was encouraged to attend college by an English teacher. She wanted to go to college, but first she needed to save some money, so she returned to teaching.

Personal tragedy struck when Angie came down with typhoid fever in 1915 and nearly died. Her mother nursed her back to health, saving her life. She would never forget the sacrifices her mother made, not only for her, but for the entire family. She wanted to make her mother's life easier and better and promised her as much.

When Debo recovered, she enrolled at the University of Oklahoma. After several changes of majors, she settled on history. Her instructor, Edward Everett Dale, wanted his students to share his enthusiasm for the history taking place around them. In Debo, he had an apt student. Under his tutelage she learned not only research techniques and a new writing style, but about the Indians, pioneers, traders, and cattlemen who would change Oklahoma's landscape. In 1918, Debo earned her bachelor's degree in history.

After graduation, she was principal in Enid and then taught students at Enid High School for four years before heading to the University of Chicago, where she received her master's degree. Her thesis, "The Historical Background of the American Policy of Isolation," was published in *Smith College Studies in History* in 1924.

Debo applied to twenty-nine universities to teach history. All twenty-nine rejected her. Determined to teach, Debo took a job in Canyon, Texas, at the West State Teachers' College and stayed there from 1924 to 1933. This training school prepared students to teach children from kindergarten to tenth grade. Debo taught general education classes. Throughout this time, Debo hoped for a promotion and move to the history department, but it never came. Some thought her assertiveness and businesslike manner held her back. After all, women weren't supposed to speak their minds and speak out boldly on issues.

During these nine years, however, Debo had good times too. *Farm and Family* published a story Debo wrote titled "The Right Kind of Wisdom," for which she was paid $160. She also wrote about the Comanche and Cherokee Indians and had several pieces published in the *Panhandle Plains Historical Review,* the *Southwest Review,* and the *Southwestern Historical Quarterly.* Her fascination with Indian history continued to grow as did her concern. She saw through tribal records, speeches by Indian leaders, court documents, and other archive material that the Indians were not being treated fairly or honestly by the government.

Debo briefly returned home to Marshall to help her sister-in-law and parents nurse her ailing brother, Edwin. He died of Hodgkin's disease on October 3, 1931. After his funeral, Debo returned to Texas.

While teaching in Canyon, she enrolled in the PhD program at the University of Oklahoma and in the fall studied again under Dr. Dale for three more years. In 1933, Debo completed her dissertation and received her doctorate. While working on her dissertation, Dale suggested some new areas of research. It was during one of those research forays to Muskogee, Oklahoma, that she met Grant Foreman and his wife, Carolyn. These two historians would become Debo's lifelong friends.

Shortly after her dissertation was completed, she found West Texas Teacher's College would not renew her employment contract. Not understanding why she was passed over again and why a less qualified woman would be taking over the position she wanted, Debo went to S. A. Hill, President of West Texas College and protested. After all, she now had a PhD. Hill appointed her curator of the Panhandle Plains Museum, and thus began a time for research.

During the next year, 1934, she expanded her dissertation, and it was published by the University of Oklahoma Press as *The Rise and Fall of the Choctaw Republic*. The book received the John H. Dunning Prize of the American Historical Association, which included a two-hundred-dollar monetary award. The book received mostly favorable reviews, but it did receive a scathing review in the *Chronicles of Oklahoma* from Muriel H. Wright, a member of the Oklahoma Historical Society and granddaughter of Choctaw Chief Allen Wright.

"The text of Miss Debo's volume is inadequate and superficial in many places due to her unfamiliarity with Choctaw affairs and hurried research," Wright wrote. "Its prejudiced viewpoints and inaccurate statements will leave misleading, even wrong impressions which will make it difficult for the reader unacquainted with the Choctaws to gain a fair estimate of them and their history."

The review disappointed Debo, but with her book doing well she decided to overlook it. After all, she had done her research. She knew the information she had found and included was correct. Her approach to interpreting American Indian history was unique because of her honesty. She wouldn't defend the facts she found. She would only write about them. From early on her motto was "to discover the truth and publish it." It didn't matter who she came across in her research, elected official or Joe Blow down the street. If they were found to be exploiting Native Americans for personal gain, she wrote about them. From that she would never back down. To her, shrinking from her responsibility to be honest would be the worst form of bigotry.

The success of that book, spurred her into two decisions. First, she quit her job in Texas, and at the age of forty-four moved back in with her parents to start another book, *And Still the Waters Run*. That work was made possible through a grant from the Social Science Research Council. A back bedroom became her new office. The book was finished in 1936. She considered this the most important work of her career. She was not one to use secondary sources. Dale had discouraged that when she was in his classes. Debo's research and knowledge was gained through primary sources, oral history, tribal records, government documents, and court records to name a few.

While doing research she found injustices and conspiracies running rampant through the government against the Indians. Writing this book was both disheartening and eye-opening. She once commented that if she knew what she was going to uncover, she wouldn't have taken on the task. The book was about the Five Civilized Tribes and how they had been cheated by grafters, state and federal governments, and ultimately by American conquest, imperialism, and progress. She wrote about how they were cheated out of their lands by the federal government and its forced liquidation plans.

Debo immediately sent the manuscript to the University of Oklahoma Press where it met with great reviews from first readers and scholars. Floyd A. Wright, a law professor at the University of Oklahoma, called it a "masterpiece." However, Debo was warned that she needed to tone down some parts. Those who read it were afraid of libel suits because of the names she named, such as former Governor Charles N. Haskell and Robert L. Owen, a former senator.

Many of the people named were donors to the university and with the university press being so new, school officials were afraid funds would be cut off. The director, Joseph A. Brandt, wanted to publish Debo's book, but after the two discussed it, they decided to dissolve the contract and Debo withdrew her submission. It would be many years before the book was published. In 1938, when Brandt moved to Princeton and became the Princeton University Press director, he requested that Debo send the manuscript to him there. *And Still the Waters Run* was published by Princeton University Press two years later.

Debo worked on a book about the Creek Indians, *The Road to Disappearance,* as she also had gained new employment, this time as the director for Oklahoma's State Writers' Project funded by the Works Projects Administration (WPA) in April 1940. She worked with a group of forty writers who were to research and conduct interviews to record Oklahoma's history. The work, when finished, would be a state guide book. While perhaps the writers could research and interview, their writing skills were lacking, and Debo found herself correcting mistakes much like a school teacher corrects the mistakes of her pupils. Debo brought the same research and work ethic she had aspired to since graduation to this job and expected the writers under her guidance to live up to those standards. When they didn't, she wrote reprimands telling them exactly what she thought was wrong and how the matter could be resolved, as in a letter written on January 16, 1941.

> *I have tried constantly to impress you with the necessity of exercising care in your research. I have returned—literally—hundreds of errors in your manuscripts to you for corrections. For the first several months, I hoped that I could teach you by this method to carry out dependable research, but you have shown no improvement. . . . The '418' which I finally issued, date January 10, 1941, represents a determination on my part to compel an improvement in your work. If your improvement is immediate and complete, I shall value you accordingly.*

While she was tough, she was also fair, giving the writers under her care chances and opportunities to improve their work if they would.

Disillusioned by meetings, memos, and Washington bureaucracy, Debo resigned her position in 1941.

While working as director she heavily edited all the manuscripts turned in to her. She also wrote an essay for the project, which was published by the University of Oklahoma Press, titled *Oklahoma: A Guide to the Sooner State*. When the book was released in 1942, Debo was disappointed to find her essay had been changed without her permission. There were errors and the overall message Debo tried to present was not there.

Debo was determined not to let her past connection—good and bad—with the WPA hinder the work she saw as worthy. After all, her third book, *The Road to Disappearance*, was out and she turned her attention to working on a book about Tulsa, its history, and what made it great. She had an immense amount of research left over from her Creek book, and with the insights she gained from the WPA interviews, she felt a book on Tulsa and its oil boom would be a project worth doing. Once again, she presented history as she saw it. In 1943, the University of Oklahoma Press published *Tulsa: From Creek Town to Oil Capital*.

While writing books about history, particularly Indian history, was her passion, Debo wanted a change of pace from the controversy that had come with naming names in her past books; she wanted a change of pace. She started writing a fictional work about her home town, Marshall, calling it *Prairie City*. Using fictional names, she recounted a time in history that Debo knew well—her time. Because of its historical backdrop, she received a grant from the Alfred A. Knopf publishing house. This allowed her to work on the book without the prospect of starving.

Knopf published *Prairie City: The Story of an American Community*. The happiness she felt at its release was mingled with grief when Debo's father died at the age of eighty-one on May 15, 1944. He was reading the book and wasn't quite finished. Slowly recovering from the loss of her father, at the age of fifty she began teaching history at Marshall High School. Almost a year later she resigned, having received a fellowship from the Rockefeller Foundation to write another book about Oklahoma. With her mother growing frailer, in late 1944 she rented an apartment in Stillwater and moved there with her mother so she could be close by as she did research at Oklahoma's A&M University library. Debo had been teaching at the college off and on for some time and was offered a full-time position. She declined that position and was offered another job as curator of maps at the college. Debo felt the curator job, compared to teaching, would allow her more time to research.

While she had been struggling to find teaching jobs most of her life, now in her fifties she admitted that although she loved teaching, she loved writing more. With the Oklahoma book finished in late 1948, Debo waited anxiously for reader comments. They were not favorable. Readers felt she was being too critical, not only of their government, but in some cases Oklahomans' human nature. After discussion with her old mentor Dale, she made revisions and changed the title of the book to *Oklahoma: Foot-Loose and Fancy-Free*. In 1949, it was published by the University of Oklahoma Press. She didn't like the final printed version because many editorial changes had been made, but was honored when Oklahoma A&M honored her for the release of her new book and her contribution to history.

As her mother's health continued to decline, Debo turned her attention to not only taking care of her, but trying to find a publisher for a report she did on the conditions of the Five Civilized Tribes for the Indian Rights Association and a book on Cowboy Oliver Nelson that she edited.

On November 16, 1950, she was inducted into the Oklahoma Hall of Fame. While the induction was an honor, Debo was in no mood to celebrate. The difficulty in getting her books published, her friend and colleague Grant Foreman's health decline, and her mother's ill health played on her mind.

Her report on the Five Civilized Tribes would finally be published in pamphlet form by the Indian Rights Association located in Philadelphia.

She continued to attend functions and tried to write when she could. Between caring for her mother and trying to visit her friends, the Foremans, Debo was overwhelmed. With Grant Foreman in such poor health, and her mother suffering from dementia and diabetes, it was all Debo could do to write articles here and there.

Good news arrived in the mail in April 1952: Oliver Nelson's memoirs, titled *The Cowman's Southwest,* would be published by Arthur C. Clark the following year. Then tragedy struck: Grant Foreman died in April 1953, and a few months later Debo was forced to put her mother in a nursing home. On June 11, 1954, her mother passed away.

Without any immediate family, friends and her activist work became increasingly important to her. In the summer of 1955, she began traveling, speaking in churches about Indian affairs, sharing her research, and asking those in attendance to write their congressmen and protest the treatment of the Indians, not only in Oklahoma now, but across the west in the termination policy the government had enacted. She started a letter-writing campaign, and she herself wrote to the Secretary of the Interior, the Bureau of Indian Affairs, and even magazines and newspapers to let people know about the injustice done to the Indians and their plight. At one point she even testified before Congress because she was considered an Indian affairs expert.

Having retired to Marshall some years earlier she was honored when the city created Angie Debo Recognition Day on March 28, 1958. As friends around her continued passing away, a serenity fell on Debo, and she was happy with her life if not her government. She took time to teach a history course now and then at Oklahoma A&M. With the extra money she now had, she decided to travel to countries outside the United States and travel she did. She went to England, France, East and West Germany, Poland, Finland, Russia, and Mexico. From these travels she learned the United States wasn't the only country suffering from imperialism and human rights catastrophes.

As she grew older, she continued her fight against bigotry and injustice, joined the American Civil Liberties Union, and continued her letter-writing campaign encouraging thousands of others to join her. Over her lifetime, she wrote eleven books, edited three, collaborated on one, and wrote over one hundred articles and reviews on Indian history. Her last book, *Geronimo,* received the Wrangler Award from the Western Heritage Association of the National Cowboy Hall of Fame.

Debo passed away on Sunday, February 21, 1988, at St. Mary's Hospital in Enid, Oklahoma, at the age of ninety-eight. She had lived, researched, and written, her way. Even though she never held a history professor position she became a premier and respected historian. Michael D. Green, national historian, said, "[Debo's] analysis of Creek history remains the standard by which other scholars must measure their work." She won the Award for Scholarly Distinction, recognition of lifetime achievement from the American Historical Association in 1987 and her portrait hangs in the rotunda at the Oklahoma State Capitol.

Today, when Oklahomans think of Debo they think of her as *the* historian of Oklahoma, human rights advocate, activist, and guardian of Civil Liberties. Oklahoma historian Arrell Gibson described her as a "pioneer in western and American Indian history."

RACHEL CAROLINE EATON

(1869–1938)

CHAMPION FOR THE CHEROKEE

What does it take for one to be remembered through history? Must one become president or be involved in a great war? What great feats must be accomplished for one's life to be acknowledged? Perhaps it's not the big things that set people apart, but the small things steadily done over a lifetime. While many may not know who Rachel Caroline Eaton is, those researching the Cherokee nation will have come across her work. For those she encouraged to become educated or to continue their education, there is a deep appreciation of her achievements and influence.

Rachel Caroline Eaton was an educator and through her written work will continue to be one through generations. Whether for her classroom teaching or her work educating people about her Cherokee Nation, even in today's modern society, she is and will be remembered.

Rachel Caroline Eaton, affectionately known as "Callie" by friends and family, was born on July 7, 1869, four years after the Civil War ended, near Flint Creek in the Cherokee Nation. The location is just west of Maysville, Arkansas. Callie was the oldest child of George Washington Eaton and Nancy Elizabeth Ward Williams. She had three brothers and a sister, Martha "Mattie" Pauline, whom she remained close to her entire life. Her father, who was born in Texas, served in the Confederate Army during the Civil War. Her mother, who was part Cherokee, was named after Callie's grandmother, who had been removed from her ancestral homeland and came to Oklahoma on the Trail of Tears.

Callie's family settled in Claremore Mound, near Claremore, Oklahoma, in Rogers County in 1874. That is where she spent time as a little

Rachel Caroline Eaton Courtesy of Martha Berry

girl. Here, she learned about her ancestors, the struggles of the Cherokee Nation, and learned firsthand the cruelty and unfair practices of the US government. While she was always loyal to her country, she knew not to trust the men who ran it.

Her parents came to the Cherokee Nation in Indian Territory and homesteaded an area of over a thousand acres. By the time's standard, the family was well off. They had cattle, raised crops to sell, had bees for honey, and lived a comfortable life in their big two-story house with a large front porch. When the government decided they wanted more land for white settlers, the family's land allotment was cut down to 120 acres. The Eaton family was luckier than most. They got to keep the land where the big house sat, and their land still had the stream that ran along the edge of their new property line. The family never starved, but their assets were cut down to only twelve percent of what they were and they never could recover what was lost.

Growing up, she had heard the stories of her ancestors, and her interest in history, particularly Cherokee history, began at an early age. It probably seemed strange that the heritage her family and friends wanted to preserve wasn't talked about in the school she attended.

Callie began her formal early education in the Cherokee Nation's tribal schools, and then when she was old enough, she attended the Cherokee Female Seminary at Park Hill, Oklahoma. She wasn't a straight-A student, but she adopted the culture of the seminary early on and continued to live in its new ways. In other words, she learned to be white. Cherokee leaders felt their people had a lot to make up and strive for if they were to keep pace with the white man. Because they felt they had been cheated by the white man because of their ignorance in many areas, their goals were to educate their children so they wouldn't be taken advantage of like so many before them.

"While our neighboring Tribes and Nations are pressing forward in the pursuit of knowledge, let not the Cherokee . . . be second in the race," former Chief William Potter Ross said in a speech at the opening of the tribe's seminaries. "The last thing our tribe needs is lazy and useless men and slouchy and slip-shod women."

To make sure this didn't happen, the seminaries were given a mandate not only to educate, but to make students well-rounded citizens by requiring that chores be done, a dress code followed, and that manners and etiquette be taught and used. Each grade had its own curriculum, and students were held to high standards. Younger children studied arithmetic, composition, grammar, geography, penmanship, phonics, and reading. Older students learned botany, chemistry, English history, French, German, and philosophy, and also read the works of Homer, Goethe, and Julius Caesar. Even though the school was Cherokee, the school taught no classes in Cherokee history, language, religion, nor any other aspects of Cherokee culture. The Cherokee language was not spoken, and the English language was not only spoken, but also taught.

Classes began in August and ran through the end of May. Callie and the other students began their day at 5:30 a.m. and ended it at 9:15 p.m. They were busy: attending classes, praying in chapel, and preparing recitations. At mealtimes, the girls dressed in appropriate attire, filed into the dining room, and ate under the careful and watchful eyes of teachers or upper class women.

Callie lived and thrived in this type of environment. Always involved in church activities, she and a classmate, Bluie Adair, founded a branch of the Young Women's Christian Association. In addition to the other chapel services and devotionals, this group offered an extra weekly prayer meeting at the school. Even from an early age, Callie was a member of the Presbyterian Church. Her loyalty and devotion came from the example her grandmother, Lucy Ward Williams, who became deeply involved with the Presbyterian Church. Callie's devotion was so deep, in fact, that her friends and family thought she might become a missionary.

Perhaps she considered it. As graduation grew near she was undoubtedly assessing her skills and planning her future. She now knew how to speak, read, dress, and carry herself like a lady, and make the Cherokee nation proud. While she and the two other girls who made up her graduating class were excited about their last year, an incident happened that dampened their spirits and affected the future life that Callie was so eagerly awaiting.

In 1887, Easter Sunday morning, a fire burned the girls' seminary building to the ground. A man by the name of Louis McLain often visited the seminary. He tried repeatedly to get the girls to go into the woods with him, so he could allegedly "preach the gospel" to them and save their souls. On this particular morning, on one of his strange visits, embers lifted from his pipe and drifted toward an open window, where they lighted on the curtains and caught fire. When the boys from the male seminary and the townspeople saw the smoke, they immediately came to help, but high winds and lack of nearby water made their efforts futile, and the building burned to the ground, along with most of its records. Callie understood that all the history of her beloved institution was gone, and she learned that day what it was like to experience true loss. She would later vow to preserve Cherokee Nation history so that it might avoid a similar fate.

That night, the girls were put up in the homes of residents from surrounding towns and in available rooms in the male seminary. The next morning, Callie began her hour-and-a-half trek home. While many of the female students had to enroll in other schools to continue their education, Callie and her two classmates were lucky enough to receive their diplomas with ten male graduates on June 28, 1888.

A new seminary was built at Tahlequah and opened a year after Callie graduated. She would return years later to teach at this new school under someone she admired.

After graduation, Callie headed east to Drury College in Springfield, Missouri, where she received her bachelor of science degree. It wasn't unusual for the girls from the seminary to attend the college. Many students from the Indian Territories wound up going to Drury. While she had always had a penchant for history, it was Professor Edward M. Sheppard who encouraged her to study Indian history, a field of study that would engage her longtime interest. She then went on to the University of Chicago, where she received her master's and doctorate in history.

When Callie finished her education, she taught in the Cherokee Nation public schools. One place that was near and dear to her heart was the Cherokee Female Seminary, now located in Tahlequah, Oklahoma. Even though the location had changed, the seminary still instilled the same moral and ethical values Callie had been brought up with and the educational standards she had come to respect. She served there for two years: 1896 through 1897. Through the years, she would be head of the history department for the State College for Women in Columbia, Missouri; history professor in Painesville, Ohio, at Lake Erie College; and dean of women at Trinity University in San Antonio, Texas.

Besides teaching, Callie had another love—writing. She knew that to preserve her love and respect for the Cherokee Nation, its stories needed to be written down. For her dissertation topic she chose Cherokee history; it was entitled "John Ross and the Cherokee Indians."

"The aim of this historical sketch is to trace the evolution from barbarism to civilization of one of the most progressive tribes of North American Indians; to give a sympathetic interpretation of their struggle to maintain their tribal identity and ancestral domains against the overwhelming tide of economic development advancing from the Atlantic seaboard westward." Another aim of the work, as Callie wrote in the forward of her paper, was "to relate the story of their forcible removal to the western wilderness where in the midst of hard-won prosperity they were plunged into the horrors of the Civil War."

Later, her dissertation was expanded into a manuscript that was published in 1914 by the George Banta Publishing Company of

Menasha, Wisconsin. It was a huge success. Used frequently as a history book for schools and colleges, it continues to be the authoritative text for researchers, who respect the research that produced it and know that its historical content is priceless because Callie had access to people others didn't.

The book covered not only the history of the Cherokee Nation, and its importance to the United States, but also the history of how John Ross became the Cherokee's chief. That story began in the early eighteenth century when the white man began encroaching on the continent and Indians struggled to hold their people together. When the Civil War broke out, Chief Ross tried to keep his people neutral in the conflict, thinking it would save them grief in the future. But it was not to be. The young men of the tribe were drawn into the conflict, and another dark period in the Cherokee Nation.

"Miss Carolyn Eaton's book is a history of the Cherokee Nation from the beginning of the 18th century to the end of the 19th," a supporter, Mrs. Sam, wrote to James Thoburn in regards to getting the book added to the Oklahoma historical collection. "It is social, economic, and political in nature stressing the rapid advancement [the Cherokee] made in the arts of civilization and the phenomenal effect upon the tribe of Sequoyah's alphabet. It is *not* biographical in the sense that Emmet Starr's book is nor does it give lengthy quotations from source material as some Oklahoma authors do. She has gleaned much material, firsthand, from many prominent men and women of the Cherokee tribe of which she is a member. She has had the privilege of seeing and hearing all of the principal chiefs of the nation since the Civil War."

After the book was published in the 1920s, she served two consecutive terms as superintendent of public instruction of Rogers County in northeastern Oklahoma. As her education role continued, so did her research and writing; however, she wasn't able to devote the time she wanted to her writing until her retirement.

In 1930 she wrote an essay for the General Federation of Women's Clubs titled "The Legend of the Battle of Claremore Mound, Oklahoma." It was published in the Federation's booklet in October 1930 as *Traditional Background of the Indians.* Callie was an excellent source for the piece as her family's property backed up to Claremore Mound, and as a youngster Callie would have played around the site and visited it often. The family told stories about tourists coming through the area asking permission to visit the mound and hunt for arrowheads.

Callie was married for a brief time, but no children came of the union. The marriage was so short-lived, as a matter of fact, that even though her husband's name is known, nothing else is known about James Alexander Burns. The year of her marriage is also a mystery, although some believe the couple married shortly after she graduated from Drury College and were separated before she started studies for her master's degree. Callie remained single for the rest of her life, devoting herself to the educational field and her writing.

She kept herself busy in her community through clubs and organizations such as the Tulsa Indian Women's Club, a branch of the Oklahoma Federation of Women's Clubs, and Eastern Star. She also became involved with her sister's children, taking a nephew under her wing and making sure he had a place to stay in Tulsa while he completed his education.

Life never was easy for her. After she retired, she began work on another manuscript, *The History of the Cherokee Indians.* She was also diagnosed with breast cancer. While she worked feverishly on the manuscript, her one desire was to live long enough to finish it. She called her nephew to her on her deathbed and asked one favor, that he guard the manuscript and make sure it got published. Callie believed in exposing truths in her work, so she knew there would be opposition to what she had written. But she wanted the truth to be known. Through the years, the manuscript has been mailed out and rejected and passed down through generations. Almost eighty years later, the family is pursuing publication again.

In 1936, Callie was inducted into the Oklahoma Memorial Association's Hall of Fame as one of Oklahoma's most outstanding women. She died in Claremore, Oklahoma, on September 20, 1938, after a long but brave battle with breast cancer.

Although she is gone, her legacy lives on in the form of her books and articles. Anyone who wants to really understand Oklahoma and its Indians has but to pick up Callie's books and read them. She and her work will not be forgotten.

ELVA SHARTEL FERGUSON

(1869–1947)

JOURNALIST IN THE GOVERNOR'S MANSION

There are those people who observe history, some who write about it, and some who make it. Elva Shartel Ferguson did all three. From prairie wife to reporter to Oklahoma Territory first lady, she saw history and became a part of it. Few can report that claim to fame.

As a little girl, Elva Shartel Ferguson had no idea that she'd travel a difficult road in life. But when obstacles came, only once did she consider quitting a task, and when that happened, she just straightened her spine and carried on in true pioneer fashion. Her resilience carried her all the way to the Oklahoma governor's mansion, and even now, years after her death, she is held in high esteem by Oklahomans who get to know her through writings about her and what she wrote about herself.

Born on April 6, 1869, in Novelty, Missouri, to David E. and Mary Jane Wiley Shartel, Elva had an advantage many other women didn't and wouldn't have. Her father was superintendent of schools, so she was educated in the public schools at Novelty. She met and married Thompson B. Ferguson in Sedan, Kansas, in 1885. Being close to Indian Territory, the couple participated in three land runs, finally settling permanently in Watonga, then part of Oklahoma Territory, in 1892.

At the age of twenty-three, on an early, cool, rainy October morning in 1892, she drove a covered wagon packed with the young family's household goods and some camping supplies. One of her small sons rode by her side, while her baby son rode on her lap. Her husband drove another wagon, which held the press they had been using in Sedan, plus type and printing supplies for the new newspaper they would be running in their new town. It would be called the *Watonga Republican*.

Elva Shartel Ferguson Courtesy of the Research Division of the Oklahoma Historical Society, Oklahoma City

Elva was not impressed with her new hometown when the family arrived, shortly after nightfall on October 1, 1892. The muddy streets and the sounds of whooping and hollering from the brightly lit saloons did not give the young mother confidence in the place where she wanted to raise her sons.

"Drunken revelry from these places made me shudder and I looked at the sleeping babe on my lap, and at the small boy at my side, resolving that I would not raise my boys in such a wild place," Shartel wrote in her book, *They Carried the Torch*. "In the morning," she told her husband, "we're going back to Kansas."

But when morning arrived, T. B. had convinced her to stay. They had been asked to go to Watonga by the Watonga Republicans to balance out the Democrat factions with a dose of Republican reality. T. B. had been editing the *Sedan Republican* in Sedan, Kansas, for years, so his work was known. In the family's new hometown, he would edit the new paper, the *Watonga Republican*.

As Elva helped him unpack their belongings and the press into the ten-dollar-a-month building he rented, she was sure to still have trepidations. The press was to occupy the lower and front part of the building because it had the best light, while the family living quarters would occupy the rest of the building.

The next morning, while Elva cooked breakfast, she turned to see a Cheyenne Indian in full regalia and a painted face standing in the doorway. She gave a whoop, scaring the Indian away, and causing her husband to run to her aid. They later discovered the Indian had heard of the new family arriving in town and came to see them out of curiosity. The family and the Indian later became best friends.

Elva learned to adjust quickly to unusual events in the rowdy frontier town. While the *Watonga Republican* was making its mark on the town and area, competing not only against a rival newspaper, the *Watonga Rustler,* but making enemies of town establishments like the saloons,

Elva came to love the community newspapers. She contributed to the running of the paper by setting type and writing the occasional socialite article. Her husband wrote about lawlessness in their growing town and incensed many of the town's business owners.

Several months after they had opened the doors to their paper, Elva had to adjust even further. One night, while the family was having dinner, a couple of cowboys rode down Noble Avenue, where the newspaper and Ferguson home were located, and fired shots into the newspaper office, barely missing a family member and Elva herself, who had stood up to serve the family supper. After surveying the scene to make sure everyone was unharmed, she filled plates, sat back down at the table, and the final meal of the day continued.

On another cold night, the Fergusons had retired to bed when they were awakened by a fire someone set to their home. They barely escaped with their lives. The culprit was soon apprehended and he confessed readily to the crime, stating that a saloon owner had given him ten dollars and a bottle of whiskey to "burn the editor" out of town.

That Christmas though, with everything going on, Elva was more than homesick. She remembered the Christmases back in Kansas, with their family dinners and presents. In their new home, they hadn't had time, money, or resources to think about the holiday. Now that it was upon them, Elva felt desperation for their lack. A knock came at the door, and when Elva opened it, it wasn't Santa, but it could have been. It was the local baker, carrying a huge basket full of everything they needed to make Christmas special.

As the town grew, so did the reputation of the Fergusons. They were known as able, honest, and capable citizens. As Republicans, they were involved in the politics of the day, and as newspaper owners were able to voice their opinions more loudly than other citizens. But as in all pioneer towns, money was in scarce supply. In her book, Elva wrote about the newspaperman's plight: "There was little money in western Oklahoma.

It was an agricultural country and market prices for what little could be raised on new soil were very low. Editors sent their newspapers to their subscribers in exchange for corn, butter, eggs, potatoes, in fact any commodity that could be used by the editor's family."

Community newspapers were always hoping to get added revenue from city and county printing contracts, but those seemed few and far between. A national-level job sometimes given to editors of community newspapers was that of postmaster. In 1897 Ferguson was appointed to this position. He moved the fourth-class post office to the front of the printing building, and for two years the family operated the additional business. Ferguson resigned after those two years, claiming that holding the federal job interfered with his political activities.

After his resignation, Elva began taking on more of a role with the paper. While her husband was away in Guthrie fulfilling his duties as territorial chairman of the Republican Party, she not only took care of her two sons and did her housekeeping duties, but also wrote the editorials for the paper, set the type, and managed the newspaper. Because of her misgivings at that time, knowing that "women were not believed to have the intellect required for the intricate job of writing editorials, particularly political ones," she wrote: "If the *Republican* is not quite up to standards these days the people will please understand that during the absence of the senior editor, the work of editing and managing of the paper devolves entirely upon the junior editor who is somewhat of an amateur in editorial writing." But the paper did not suffer during her husband's absences, and in truth this time of her life proved to be a turning point.

As Watonga prospered, so did the paper and the Fergusons' fortune. They added new equipment to the business, and in 1901 had a three-story Victorian home constructed, complete with white picket fence, on the east side of town. Elva loved her new home, and the family settled in nicely. T. B. expanded the family business to include another newspaper twelve miles north of Watonga in a little town called Hitch-cock. In November, it was on one of his trips to Hitchcock to write, print, and distribute his new weekly newspaper, the *Hitchcock Vanguard,* that events occurred that would change the family forever.

While he was gone Elva had stayed behind to take care of business at the *Republican* as usual. When Theodore Roosevelt became president in September 1901, after the assassination of President McKinley earlier that month, he turned his attention to getting a new Territorial Governor in place. He called a delegation of prominent Oklahomans to Washington and asked for their opinion on who he should appoint. Several names were offered, but were rejected because of one issue or another.

The president, perplexed and annoyed, finally asked the delegation, "Is there not one honest man in the whole territory upon whom I can depend, who has nerve and a backbone necessary to make a success of the job?" One of the delegates spoke up and said he knew of such a man, a red-headed editor in western Oklahoma. After some discussion, the president was impressed with what he'd heard. He sent T. B. Ferguson a telegram.

Elva was the one who received it. In her book she writes about how the decision was made.

> *I decided that I wanted him [T. B.] to be governor, so answered the telegram at once saying he would accept and would leave by the first train for Washington. I bought his railroad ticket, had his traveling bag packed and everything ready for his departure when he reached home late that evening.*
>
> *After he read the telegram and the answer I had sent, he declined to accept and said that since I had acted without his con-sent that I could send another telegram saying he did not want the job. But I had not come in contact with his Scotch stubborn-ness for years without learning how to manage in such cases, so*

he went to Washington as I had planned, got the approval of the President and secretary of the interior, returning home with the commission in his pocket.

What her words do not tell is that the entire town heard the loud discussion they had about the appointment. Even though they lived on the edge of town, they were only about three or four blocks from downtown Watonga. According to local historians, he didn't want the job because he didn't think he was qualified. Elva felt he was the best man for the job.

In true Elva Ferguson fashion, she didn't back down and by January 20, 1902, the family relocated to Guthrie, Oklahoma, to take up residence in the Territorial Capitol. It was not an easy time at the turn of the twentieth century. Early on there were criticisms of the newly appointed governor. Elva wrote, "Some openly said that a country editor from the sticks did not know enough about statecraft to be a successful governor. Politicians did not like him because they knew they could not use him."

Elva was always on and by his side. During the social season, she was the one who made sure he was dressed properly. She recalled, "It took a great of diplomacy on my part to get him into his dress suit and have him in attendance at the social affairs which the governor and his wife were obliged to favor with their presence." She also stepped in to make sure anything that wasn't going well was taken care of immediately. After all, she didn't want her family to be remembered as country people from the sticks, and she took on roles to make sure that didn't happen.

During the years her husband was in office, she wrote about what was going on in the Indian Territorial Capitol for the *Watonga Republican* back home. When her husband was ill, she took over his role in the governor's office, writing letters for him and signing her own name to them. At other times, she didn't balk from strapping on an apron and helping out wherever she could.

Such an incident happened when the Secretary of the Interior Ethan Allen Hitchcock and several other Washington officials were coming to the Territory to inspect various institutions that were under the Interior's jurisdiction. A reception was held from three to five o'clock in the afternoon, in which the first lady was to stay in attendance, and then later they would go to the governor's home for dinner. Elva had hired extra help to assist her cook, and because arrangements had been made in advance, she was sure everything would be ready. Elva recalled what happened next in the pages of her book.

"During my absence at the reception a general knock-down and drag out scrap had taken place among my help and my cook.

"When I reached home at five o'clock the house was deserted, not a negro in sight and very little done toward the dinner. Of course, I was almost frantic. Telephone calls to some of my friends soon brought an experienced cook from the home of one of them to take charge, and another good friend found trained waiters for me and another came personally to my rescue. We took off our party dresses, put on our aprons and were soon at work in the kitchen, bringing order out of chaos."

Of course, when the guests finally arrived an hour later, Elva was back in her party dress meeting the dignitaries with a smile. No one knew of the catastrophe in the kitchen and the dinner party was hailed a success.

During their time in Guthrie, the Ferguson administration made some sweeping changes. Ferguson improved conditions at the insane asylum, signed herd laws that required ranchers to fence their property so their cattle wouldn't destroy farmers' crops, and he signed a bill which allowed osteopath doctors the right to practice their skills in Oklahoma.

Elva saw these changes as a step in the right direction for Oklahoma. She knew her husband made a lot of enemies, but always forward thinking, she was proud of the work they did while in office and the way they represented Oklahoma Territory.

When their term was over, they returned to Watonga and the paper. In 1914, she became editor of a society page and added a column of her own titled "Just Remarks." While those on the outside may have seen Elva as a strong woman who had it all, that strength came from adversity. She and her husband had five children, three girls and two boys. Only the two boys survived to adulthood and on January 19, 1919, her youngest son, Tom "Trad" Ferguson died of pneumonia at Fort Sill.

Many felt that Trad's death hastened his father's. As his illness grew, Elva took over almost all the business of running the *Republican*. When T. B. passed away on February 14, 1921, she took over complete control of the newspaper. The editor's chair and editorials were all hers, and she editorialized to her heart's content.

Never one to sit around and become stagnant, in 1924 she served as chair of the state delegation to the Republican National Convention. In 1926, she represented Oklahoma at the Philadelphia Sesquicentennial Exposition. Elva always promoted the interests of Oklahoma and had done so since 1904, when she supported her husband's initiative to have Oklahoma represented at the St. Louis World's Fair. It was both her and T. B.'s desire to have Oklahoma Territory become a state. They were both pleased when statehood happened shortly after they left office.

From 1928 to 1933, Elva served as vice-chair of the State Republican Committee. During these years many changes came into her life. She met the writer Edna Ferber, who spent time with Elva learning about the pioneer spirit, Oklahoma, the *Republican*, and Elva's life in general. In 1930, when Elva sold her interest in the newspaper business and retired, Ferber published her book, *Cimarron*. The book, which was based on Tom and Elva's lives, was made into a movie by RKO Studios in the '30s, and Elva became the technical advisor for the newspaper print shop scenes. The movie was nominated for seven Academy Awards and won three—for outstanding production, best writing-adaptation, and best art direction.

Even though Elva retired from the newspaper business, she continued writing. She wrote articles on newspaper pioneers for the *Daily Oklahoman* through the 1930s and her book, *They Carried the Torch—The Story of Oklahoma's Pioneer Newspapers*, was published in 1937. The book was dedicated to her son Walter, the young boy who rode by his mother's side when they first arrived in Watonga those many years ago. Walter died on March 8, 1936, of a heart attack.

Elva received many honors toward the end of her life. She was inducted into the Oklahoma Hall of Fame in 1933, and in 1946 she was elected Oklahoma's State Mother by the American Mothers Committee of the Golden Rule Foundation in New York City. She passed away on December 18, 1947, in Watonga.

While Elva was honored by all the accolades she received, she wanted most to be remembered for her work as a pioneer newspaperwoman. In her book, she wrote, "I know of no work as fascinating as that as editor of a newspaper. . . . I hope that when I reach the golden streets of the New Jerusalem I may pitch my tent along with the other pioneer newspaper men and women of Oklahoma, where we can reminiscence [*sic*] about pioneer days without interruption from the present generation, who believe that they know better than we did how to edit a newspaper."

ANNETTE ROSS HUME

(1858–1933)

PHOTOGRAPHER, GENEALOGIST, CIVIC LEADER

People say a picture is worth a thousand words. Annette Ross Hume only knew she was capturing her town, the people around her, and moments in her life with her camera. Little did she know that someday her photographic hobby would serve as a record of a time gone by and of a town and a state coming into their own. And while this Oklahoman may be best known for her photographs, her life was a large one, encompassing much more. She was a frontierswoman, wife, mother, churchgoer, community and civic leader, and genealogy historian. Her motto was "home must come first, and then give all the aid you can in building up civic and patriotic organizations."

Annette Ross Hume was born on March 18, 1858, in Perrysburg, Ohio, in Wood County. Her parents were James White Ross and Katherine Darling Ross. She was the eldest daughter of the couple. Her father was mayor and councilman of their little town, and he also operated a small subscription school in the town's courthouse. Her mother's brother was a member of the Perrysburg Board of Education and was instrumental in getting the first public school built there. It was only natural that Annette received her education at the Perrysburg High School. She graduated at the age of sixteen as valedictorian in 1874.

In her diary of 1876, she writes about teaching school at Perrysburg and about a suitor, Charles Robinson Hume, who was a young doctor practicing in their local county. Hume had received his medical degree from Michigan University in 1874. The couple was married two days after Christmas on December 27, 1876, at her parent's home.

Annette Ross Hume Courtesy of the Research Division of the Oklahoma Historical Society, Oklahoma City

Shortly after their marriage, they moved to a little town in Ohio, Tontogany. While there, they had two sons, Carlton Ross and Raymond Robinson. The growing family did not stay long in Ohio. By the 1880s they had moved to a cattle town on the frontier called Caldwell. A Kansas town, it sat right along the southern border of the state line and was the last town travelers came to before crossing over into Indian Territory. It was also a stopping and loading point for cattle driven along the Chisholm Trail. Cowboys, Indians, gunmen, lawmen, saloons, and the railroad converged there to make Caldwell notorious for its violence and lawlessness.

Annette's husband, Dr. Hume, kept busy there serving the town and surrounding area. Her brother, Henry Addison Ross, moved to Caldwell also, and then in 1883, her parents and other siblings joined them in the rough and dangerous town. While she was glad to have her family together again, Annette suffered several personal tragedies during this time. Three more children were born to her and Charles, but they all died in infancy from malnutrition. The couple stayed in Caldwell for ten years before deciding to move on to new adventures.

Charles participated in the Oklahoma Land Run of 1889. He let Annette's sister, Celida Ross, file on the claim. Not long after he was appointed physician for the Kiowa, Comanche, and Wichita Agency by the US government. The agency was located in southwestern Indian Territory, in present-day Anadarko, Oklahoma.

He traveled ahead of the family arriving at the agency on December 1, 1890. He went back and got Annette, the children, and Celida a month later. They rode the Chicago, Rock Island and Pacific Railroad to Minco in Indian Territory, twenty miles northeast of their destination. From there, they rode a mail hack while their belongings were loaded onto a freight wagon for the trip.

They arrived on Wednesday, December 31, at 7:00 p.m. Because none of their furniture and belongings had been settled in the house yet, they stayed at the Hotel Anadarko until they could get things unpacked. The four-room wooden cottage was not fancy by any means, but Annette set about making it a home. The agency wasn't much of a settlement, but supplied everything a family might need. There were a couple of stores, a bakery, dairy, post office, jail, sawmill, blacksmith shop, carpenter shop, school, a few churches, and then the homes of the agency's employees. Beyond the agency's limits, there wasn't much else to be seen. The land was flat, and only the occasional tree graced the grounds with its presence.

Annette was not deterred in the least by her dismal surroundings. She busied herself "helping make a home for an 'object lesson' for Indians and the comfort of missionaries." Besides her household duties she immediately became involved in the community and active with the Presbyterian Church. She and her family hosted many missionaries who came through the area doing God's work.

As new forms of photography were spreading across the country, Annette became interested in the hobby. While cameras were still bulky, and the developing process was completed in steps, she was up to the challenge. Going on rounds with Dr. Hume, she took her camera along. While he checked on patients, she took pictures of the people and places around her. When not going with him, she took pictures of her neighbors and the events going on at the agency.

During this time, she was also making strides with her church activities. In the spring of 1893, she was appointed representative for the Woman's Home Mission Board. That fall she helped form the Synodical Society. The group met at Miss Alice Robertson's home. Robertson would become an Oklahoma representative in the sixty-seventh Congress. Hume served as president of the society and would do so for seven years. As such, she traveled around the country speaking and helping organize other societies. The society's purpose was to provide schools and teachers for the western and southwestern US mission field.

In 1899, she became involved with the Oklahoma State Federation of Women's Clubs. A proud moment came when, after helping form the Philomatic Club of Anadarko, it was accepted almost immediately into the Oklahoma State Federation of Women's Clubs. Her first role in the OSFWC was to serve as their parliamentarian, a position she held for eight years.

Besides the work in her church and with the state federation, Hume was also deeply involved in doing genealogic research. Besides amassing a large library, she wrote numerous letters asking for and receiving information on her family history. She was passionate about this work, and in one of her bios she included in an ad, in which she was soliciting for work, she writes, "Mrs. Hume considers herself a real American, for her maternal ancestors came from Winthrop in 1630, founded Boston, Dorchester, then removed to Connecticut where they founded Windsor, Wethersfield, Hartford, New Haven, Springfield, etc. One of the best known of these [ancestors] was Governor John Haynes, who served as Governor of Massachusetts before removing to Hartford to help form that colony, and was the first Governor of the Connecticut Colony."

Hume took her research seriously. It wasn't enough for her to hear about who might or might not be her ancestor; she always required proof, the hallmark of any serious researcher. In many of her letters, she asked other researchers to provide her with clarified information or copies and sources of any research they may have found. No doubt a Bible given to her husband by his aunt in 1896 was a place to start looking for the Humes' ancestors and may have sparked her interest in genealogy.

Hume was once asked, "What makes a book valuable—age or associations?" Her answer was, "Both." The Bible given to the Humes had been in the family and used for over two hundred years. While the Bible itself was not large—about six inches long, three inches wide and three inches thick—and had been recovered several times and was missing the first two chapters of Genesis, it was still cherished by the family. Besides its spiritual legacy, it contained a list of many marriages and births. The first entry was, "Bennet Eliot and Lettice Aggar married on 14 June 1598."

Besides searching, Annette was always sharing. On May 30, 1924, she wrote, "Lately made copies of old ROSS records for my nephew, and copied old manuscripts and records for him and kept carbons of all data, to supply others with same." She considered the quest a two-way street.

In 1901, Anadarko officially became a city. Settlers came into the city and set up tents while they waited to get registered for a chance at a homestead. The city was platted and settlers came in to get their own plot of land within the city. Annette took pictures of this great change and the ragtown that sprang up overnight. Before the campers arrived, the surrounding fields were cornfields with stalks growing tall and dry from the summer drought. Later pictures show the road formed by the influx of settlers and the stalks of corn trampled down by horses, wagons, and the bustle of people.

Annette enjoyed capturing life as it changed. She also enjoyed photographing Oklahoma's tribes. Her favorite subjects were the women and children she saw regularly and their distinct way of life. Many of her pictures show women carrying babies in cradle boards, whose distinctive beadwork indicated their tribal affiliation. She also photographed American Indian leaders like Quannah Parker and Geronimo.

As the town was changing, so were the Humes' lives. Dr. Hume resigned his position at the agency and opened a private practice. The family also left the agency home they had lived in for ten years and moved into a home in Anadarko proper. Their permanent address from then on would be 501 West Central Boulevard, Anadarko.

While Dr. Hume advanced his medical career, becoming the first health officer for Caddo County, first president of Caddo County Medical Society, and president of the state medical association, Annette was making strides of her own. She continued with her photography, but it was put on hold as she traveled to represent the Oklahoma and Indian Territories in St. Louis in 1904 on the Louisiana Purchase Committee.

In 1906, Annette's mother passed away. It was a difficult time for her, but somehow she summoned strength and moved forward. She served as parliamentarian of the Oklahoma State Federation of Women's Clubs for eight years and then secretary for three. At the end of 1911, while serving as secretary, Annette was feeling troubled as she tried to get more members to join the organization and to succeed in making the quotas for all the clubs' programs. In December, she received a letter from the chairman of the General Federation of Women's Clubs (National Organization), Mrs. Percy V. Pennybacker. She wrote, "Strike out from your vocabulary the word 'discouragement.' Oklahoma is a place for big things." The pep talk must have worked, for she was elected president of the organization by an overwhelming two-thirds vote two years later in 1913.

As president, she wanted to bring certain issues not only to the attention of Oklahomans, but to the nation as well. She wanted women's role as mothers to be respected and to improve women's educational opportunities. She saw the latter as a way to bring positive change, particularly in the health of women and their families.

In her closing speech of 1915, when she was stepping down from her presidency, she talked about these issues. Regarding motherhood, she said, "Only a mother knows the cost of a human life. Close to her heart the little one lies from the time she plans for the coming and during babyhood, while cradled in her protecting arms. Soon she trains the tiny feet to walk aright, the little tongue to speak right words, the little mind to hold pure thoughts. Then the day comes when she delegates part of the responsibility to others—but there is never a time, from the cradle to the grave, when mother ceases to bear upon her heart the welfare of her child, physical, mental, and moral."

She addressed the topic of education as well, suggesting the beneficial changes it was sure to bring: "Education is knowing what you want, where to get it, and how to use it after getting it. It is learning to do what you do not now do, rather than learning of what you do not now know. It is doing, not just knowing, that counts!"

In closing she encouraged not only the mothers, but all club women to continue to work for bettering the children and women of Oklahoma and their health conditions.

This was one area in which Annette had experience. She saw what could happen when hygiene was not followed and how diseases could swiftly travel through a family and city. She had been with her husband as he tried to help the sick and ailing and no doubt read his reports on cases of chicken pox, pneumonia, severe headaches, tuberculosis, epilepsy, bronchitis, hay fever, burns, sprains, stillbirths, and on the epidemics of malaria, measles, and smallpox.

When her work as president of the Oklahoma State Federation of Women's Clubs was finished, she continued to work with the organization in one capacity or another. "Have not missed a meeting of annual convention of the Federation for over thirty years," Annette wrote. "Have only complete file in existence of the programs and yearbooks of the State Federation, which are intended for use of the Oklahoma Historical Society to be placed in new building."

Annette continued with her genealogy work, helping organize the first state conference of the Daughters of the American Revolution (D.A.R.), which took place in Muskogee in late 1909. As a member, she once again served as parliamentarian for many years.

She spent a lot of time in her library, not only doing research in the books she had collected, but through correspondence with other genealogy resources. While tracing her own family lineage, she assisted others looking for theirs. One of her consistent goals through her genealogical work was to "aid ladies seeking to join patriotic societies." As her research successes grew and her name became known internationally, she was encouraged to join the Magna Carta Dames and other organizations of royal descent, but she declined, saying that "she cared more for what her ancestors did in America than for their deeds in Europe."

Though her successes were many, she did encounter obstacles. Many of her letters were returned with comments jotted across the bottom stating she would have to come and look for the information herself or that the person addressed in the letter didn't have time to look for her. Hume persevered and did do a fair amount of travel in her quest. When one source dried up or became unreliable, she would simply find another.

"I am doing work for several ladies whose lines run into southern states, and find it hard to get reliable information, and the genealogists employed have been dilatory, and have not given me satisfactory material for money expended, so wonder if you can give me names of researchers reliable and moderate in prices."

Her genealogy research became a small business. When asked how much she charged, this was her response: "For several years, I have had $1 an hour, plus charges for expenses in getting proofs from town clerks, etc."

Even when Dr. Hume and she began to have health problems in the late teens and early 1920s, and Annette began to lose her eyesight, she continued to write her letters of inquiry and answer those who requested information from her. She may not have responded as quickly as before, but she did still write as soon as she was able, as is recorded in this letter of May 23, 1918.

"Please pardon the unavoidable delay, for when your request came Doctor Hume was ill and we had torn up before that for repairs, so that records were inaccessible, and only yesterday were my bookcases and files put in their right places so that I could reach them again."

While her photography career ended around 1910 because of her failing health, her photos would not languish in obscurity. Edward Everett Dale, head of the history department at the University of Oklahoma learned of Annette's photographs and her large collection of glass plate negatives from her son, Carlton, a former University of Oklahoma graduate.

Annette wanted to keep her collection in the state, so after financial and preservation arrangements were made, more than 750 of her negatives were shipped to the University. They arrived in 1927 and became the central photographic core of the Phillips Collection, now the Western History Collection, at the University of Oklahoma Libraries.

Always proud of her sons, she wrote frequently about their accomplishments, from their being the first graduates at the University of Oklahoma, to their families, to their careers. In the same letter, she writes, "Our son, Sr. Carlton Ross Hume, took the examination yesterday for Medical Reserve Corps, and probably will go soon to active service, leaving a fine large practice. He has been quite successful and the community hates to see him go. Our other son, Raymond, is not quite as strong, physically and has a wife and three children, so can't well leave home, but is doing a lot of work for the Red Cross. Dr. Hume is chairman of district advisory boards and member of National Committee of Defense. He goes in a few days to Chicago as delegate to American Medical Association for our state."

In the mid-1920s things began to change again for Annette. She writes to a friend and colleague on February 3, 1928:

> *I am sorry that I have delayed replying so long, but my health has been so uncertain that mail has had to wait often. Two years ago, we were in California for three months and I had to be in a sanatorium three times for treatment for stomach trouble and heart, and have had to be careful ever since, even more than before. Am obliged to take digitalis daily and shall the rest of my life to keep heart action up.*
>
> *Often am unable to do anything for quite awhile and we spent part of the summer of 1926 and 27 in Colorado. I had such severe spells with heart last year that was in bed over three weeks and brought back in Pullman berth. Had angina pectoris, same trouble my brother died with four years ago. Had to let genealogy alone for months and am just beginning some work again.*

Through her research she writes proudly of her ancestors, the things they accomplished, the offices they held in various townships throughout the United States and of the one relative whom the family believed was a spy. "As Thomas [Darling] carried in 1744, secret messages to Benjamin Franklin (according to family traditions, when he wrote that diary, that I sent copy for your book) feel pretty sure that this letter is a cipher as there are only 6 to 8 words in a line, written big, and as I never heard of any glass industry in this family am inclined to think this is to cover up some matters . . . "

In the 1930s, she received several honors. First, she was named one of the Twenty Four Outstanding Women of Oklahoma by the Oklahoma State Federation Women's Clubs). Second, on November 15, 1930, Governor Holloway presented her with a diploma from the State Memorial Association for meritorious services. The diploma was highly prized by Hume. "These honors came unsought and as a great surprise," she wrote, "for whatever [I] have done in church, civic, educational and patriotic lines has been without thought of remuneration or even of appreciation, but just to satisfy [my] own conscience." Third, she was inducted into the Oklahoma Hall of Fame. She was grateful that the tributes were given during her lifetime.

In 1931, with her health and eyesight failing, she started the process of donating additional pictures and correspondence to the Oklahoma Historical Society. She had promised to give James Thoburn some materials, but as he was turning over his work to the society, it made sense that Hume's materials go directly to the society for preservation.

Annette Ross Hume passed away quietly in the home of her son, Dr. Raymond R. Hume, in Minco, Oklahoma, on January 19, 1933. Even though she was gone, she left behind a legacy for her family and for the state of Oklahoma. Her photographs and her letters live on and remind us of where we were and how far we have come.

In her obituary, the *Anadarko Tribune* wrote, "she was a pioneer wife active in genealogical research and patriotic work." For those who have seen her pictures or read her letters, they know she was much more.

MYRTLE ARCHER McDOUGAL

(1866–1956)

CLUBWOMAN FOR SOCIAL REFORM

Myrtle Archer McDougal was born to George Washington Archer and Sarah Jane Elizabeth Priscilla Welch Archer, on August 7, 1866, in Marietta Springs, Mississippi. Her father was a minister and town scientist, and her mother was a Southern belle. Myrtle was the couple's eighth child. Myrtle's parents surrounded their children with love, books, independence, and a challenge to think for themselves. And regularly, Myrtle's father would ask each of his children, "What have you done to justify your existence today?"

Myrtle would never forget that question and throughout her life, she lived to justify her life by helping those less fortunate than herself and by becoming a better person, personally, socially, and politically. She led an unconventional life, had unique ideas, and brought leading-edge social reforms to her home town of Sapulpa, the state of Oklahoma, and the nation.

Being an independent woman in 1883 wasn't the norm. Myrtle worked as a store clerk and then became the first female hat maker in Mississippi. She traveled throughout the state and surrounding states selling her hats, and it was on one of these trips from Baldwyn, Mississippi, to Purdy, Tennessee, that she met Donald Archibald McDougal, a young lawyer. The couple was married in Baldwyn on February 12, 1888.

They settled in Purdy, and while her husband practiced law, Myrtle took care of her home, helped her husband in the law office, and became a social force in the community. While the couple had big plans for their town, things didn't work out for them, and they soon moved to Savannah, Tennessee, where his family lived. Myrtle loved Savannah, but her

Myrtle Archer McDougal Courtesy of Special Collections, University of Miami Libraries, Coral Gables, Florida

husband had eyes for opportunities to the west. In 1893, after the financial crash, also known as the Panic of 1893, he did go west temporarily, leaving Myrtle with their three daughters. He wasn't gone long. The land run at the opening of the Cherokee Strip in Indian Territory didn't live up to his expectations, but he still thought the West was where his family could live and prosper, perhaps at another time.

While money was tight for the new family, Myrtle enjoyed life in Savannah. She had lots of energy and enthusiasm, which served her well. She sewed for others to help the family finances, took care of her children and home, took pictures, developed them in her own darkroom, and worked tirelessly for the Civil War veterans of her community through her local chapter of the Daughters of the Confederacy. She also wrote and edited the woman's edition of the local weekly newspaper, the *Savannah Courier.*

Her husband tried to settle in. He had his law practice, and when he decided to run for a circuit judgeship, Myrtle thought Savannah was where she would spend the rest of her life. It wasn't to be. When Arch lost the election after staking everything on his campaign, he decided it was time to go west again. So in 1903, he left Myrtle and the girls again in Savannah and headed back to Indian Territory. His trip stopped at a little wooden train station in Sapulpa, Creek Nation, Indian Territory.

In June 1904, Myrtle and the girls joined him there. She brought a total of twenty-five dollars, put together by one of Arch's sisters and Myrtle's family to help them get started in this new land. Myrtle was not happy about leaving Savannah, coming to a place with dirt sidewalks and meager little box houses. Her children, however, were, and even though life was difficult there, because of her husband and children's interest in their new town, she began to see that perhaps Sapulpa had possibilities after all.

After settling into their shabby little home on South Elm Street, Myrtle grew homesick and discontented with the poverty she saw all around her. She had set her house in order, and now it was time to do something else. Life in Savannah had been busy with her women's clubs and the work she was doing through them. So, if Sapulpa proper couldn't help the people around her, Myrtle Archer McDougal would. By looking around, Myrtle saw a lot that could be done.

In Savannah, Myrtle had volunteered her time to nurse her neighbors from illnesses and injuries. She would continue the practice in Sapulpa. At first, Myrtle worked with Sapulpa's citizens on a one-on-one basis. She nursed a townswoman back to health who had been badly burned from a fire explosion in her kitchen, and she helped deliver babies when she was needed.

Her middle daughter, Mary McDougal Axelson, wrote, "[Mom] taught dramatics, continued her volunteer nursing and occupied herself with church, missionary society and women's clubs' activities." Myrtle was one of two elocution teachers in town. Her students learned speeches and poems, complete with gestures, and were called on to perform throughout the community at churches, school functions, and community events regularly. In November 1904, to help her local church with its building fund, Myrtle published a women's edition of the *Sapulpa Evening Light,* the town's first newspaper.

After becoming part of the community and influenced by her husband's view that Sapulpa would be a major part of a new state, Myrtle wanted to be even more involved. They both saw the need for social, commercial, and physical reform. By contacting other southern transplanted women, Myrtle organized Sapulpa's first social club. Soon after, she founded three other organizations, the Current Events Club, a local American Red Cross Chapter, and the Thomas Wills Chapter of the Daughters of the American Revolution.

During this time a new era was being ushered in. In the East, women were forming women federation groups, and their goal was to bring about civic and legislative change across the states. In 1905, the Sapulpa women met to form their own group. Myrtle was chosen to be the representative for the newly formed (Sapulpa) Federation of Women's Clubs, and in 1906 she gave her first public address at the Indian Territory Federation of Women's Clubs convention in Tulsa. Her topic was Prohibition, something she and her husband felt passionately about. She didn't have a fancy silk and satin dress to wear, so she added a flounce of old lace to a pink—her favorite color—gingham dress.

In her speech, she made the issue personal to women. She stressed the physical, economic, and emotional toll "demon rum" took on the lives of women and children as they suffered abuse from drunken husbands and fathers. As a result of that address, the convention women passed a temperance resolution. This was the first time a women's club had taken a stand against a legislative issue that was so controversial.

On November 22, 1905, the discovery of oil southwest of town would change the family's fortunes and Sapulpa for years to come. Arch had invested in some land where black gold was found. One of the first things the family did was buy a large two-story, thirteen-room, Queen Anne house complete with tower and turret. It was located on South Oak Street not far from the shabby home on South Elm Street.

After moving into the big house, even with all her church, social work, and women's club activities, Myrtle was never one to pass up the opportunity to entertain. Her home had always been and would continue to be open to visitors. Her hospitality was well known throughout the area. Not only did friends come to the McDougals' home, but organizations held their meetings there, and on weekends the McDougals gave house parties for artists, musicians, and writers from all over the southwest.

With her interest in the arts and her organizing skills, it is no surprise she was also one of the co-organizers of the Oklahoma Author's Guild. Carrie Nation, prohibitionist, and Kate Bernard, Oklahoma's first Commissioner of Charities and Corrections, were frequent visitors to the McDougals' home as well.

By 1907, Myrtle was serving as president of the Indian Territory Federation of Women's Clubs and in 1910 she became president of the state organization, Oklahoma Federation of Women's Clubs. At this time, oil money helped the family not only take trips, but also helped Myrtle in her travels to district, regional, and national meetings and conventions of these groups.

Now she was able to dress in silk and satin, but what people remembered her for was her passion for issues and the way that passion came through in her public addresses. While women's rights were Myrtle's primary focus, she also spent time campaigning for conservation and on children and teen issues.

In an address given at the Oklahoma Federation of Women's Clubs on Wednesday evening, November 12, 1913, Myrtle said:

> *The National Conservation Congress has asked the club women to help take care of the forest. A tremendous undertaking, but we have gladly given our aid. . . . But a more valuable national asset than forest and soil is being ruthlessly wasted and sacrificed. The conservation of the forest pales into insignificance before the conservation of child life. Human figures cannot compute the loss to the state and to the nation through the large percent of preventable deaths of children in infancy. The high death rate of babies could and should be stopped.*

Besides the pure milk campaign already instituted by the women's club, Myrtle pushed for education for mothers in how to take care of their children, a health certification bill that would prevent marriages of the unfit, and the enactment and enforcement of bills that would protect women and children who worked in factories. She also strived to improve conditions for adolescent girls in Oklahoma's state schools, vocational training for young girls in public schools, and scholarships for women in state universities. Her biggest campaign and greatest success was in health reform. Under Myrtle's leadership, women studied the issues of widespread ignorance of health, sanitation, and nutritional issues in the Oklahoma frontier, gathered statistics, and lobbied people of influence to affect change. They spread the word about these issues through meetings, health brochures, and catchy slogans like "Keep Well Armies" and "Better Babies."

Besides health reform, Myrtle also brought about the establishment of libraries and recreational facilities for young people in Oklahoma. Her most controversial campaign was in women's dress. While the style was all lace and ruffles, and the trends came from Paris, she didn't consider them practical. In an address to the Oklahoma State Federation of Women's Clubs convention, Myrtle said, "It has been noised abroad that Oklahoma club women are independent enough to say to the organized dressmakers and builders of 'French creations,' 'You shall not dictate to us and force us to wear foolish, immodest and extravagant clothes. We will be a law unto ourselves and not slaves to Dame Fashion.'"

In 1907, two years after Myrtle and the girls arrived in Sapulpa, the population was 4,259. By 1910 it had almost doubled to 8,283. With the oil boom, outlaws and other unsavory elements arrived in Sapulpa. Gunfire and deaths were a daily occurrence. Brothels outnumbered churches, and people were afraid to walk down the streets alone for fear of being mugged, or worse yet, killed. Many a night, Myrtle lay in bed, listening to the chaos of the streets, wondering if her husband would return after he had been called upon to rescue someone who had been attacked or who was about to be hung. She hoped things would change after he was elected mayor and vowed to "clean up" their town. Arch had a huge following, and a number of influential citizens agreed to help him.

While her husband served as mayor of Sapulpa and worked on cleaning up its streets, Myrtle was named vice-chairman for the Oklahoma suffrage campaign. Because women's rights were her main goal, she relished the position and went to work immediately. By 1913, she had become a well-known and respected public figure whose oratory style was admired. That same year, Governor Lee Cruce appointed her an honorary Democratic committeewoman. She couldn't be a government official because the Nineteenth Amendment hadn't been passed, but she started attending conventions and became involved in party politics unofficially. That same year, she campaigned for Woodrow Wilson, and three years later Myrtle was named national director of the Wilson and Marshall League. This organization was formed to secure women's votes in the twelve suffrage states. Its goal was to send women campaigners into every nook and cranny of the western states. The League did its job, and when the votes were counted, political analysts wrote that "the western states were 'swung by the suffragettes.'"

Being a sought-after speaker, she was asked to give a speech to the Oklahoma Bar Association in 1918. She knew these men saw her in a less-than-favorable light, so right away, to set the mood, she told them of her credentials to give the address: "Having delivered nearly a quarter of a million addresses to *one* lawyer, why should my spirit faint at the thought of delivering one speech to half a thousand lawyers."

The following year, she became the national chairman for the Federation Peace Committee. This was an important and honored position for her. After all, one of the reasons she had campaigned for Woodrow Wilson was because of his world peace platform. Through this organization she instituted a national peace day and campaigned for movie censorship.

When the Nineteenth Amendment finally passed on August 18, 1920, Myrtle's volunteer position as Democratic chairwoman became an elected position. She served in that capacity for sixteen years consecutively. At the Democratic national convention that year in San Francisco, she gave two addresses nominating candidates. This was a momentous occasion for the women's movement. Even though women had spoken at conventions before, now a woman official was speaking, one whose political views carried sway in a large portion of a newly enlarged electorate. People paid attention.

Also that same year, she gave a speech at the Oklahoma State Convention of the Democratic Party. In her address on the suffrage movement she said, "It has been so short a time since I even became 'people'! But now it has become the woman's business to inform herself for the sake of home, family, children, town and nation. Women were always 100 percent Americans even when they were just 2 percent citizens."

Now that women had the right to vote, she wanted to make sure they were educated about issues when they voted so they could value their new citizenship. She wanted the Democratic Party to sponsor a program for the "newly emancipated woman" through "voter-education schools." While Myrtle laid the groundwork from Sapulpa, that same year, a new nonpartisan organization called the League of Women Voters took over the role of educating women on and about political issues.

By 1921, it was clear the Democratic Party needed to be reorganized. Myrtle was one of sixteen chosen to work on that reorganization. After her work was done, she traveled throughout the West organizing Democratic Women's Clubs. Myrtle knew how to organize clubs, and she was so successful that she was offered the position of president of the National Democratic Women's Clubs. When she was told she would have to relocate to Washington, DC, she refused the offer. She didn't want to leave her home in Sapulpa. Arch was still there practicing law and she wasn't ready to leave her home town. She continued to serve her state, however. For eighteen years she was National Democratic Committeewoman for Oklahoma.

Besides allowing the McDougals to travel, Oklahoma oil money also bought them a summer home in Florida. Even though their stay in the southeast was during the summer, Myrtle set to work organizing a social club for other Oklahomans in the area and it, like other social clubs she organized, was a huge success.

In the 1930s, the couple did go to Washington, DC. Myrtle's husband was offered a job at the Department of State under the administration of

Franklin D. Roosevelt. While Myrtle was slowing down in her official roles, she continued to be active in the National Democratic Women's Club and the National League of Pen Women. She also continued the practice of hospitality in Washington.

"[Her] luncheons, receptions, and dinners were a feature of official social life. Her guests included cabinet members, diplomats, senators, congressmen, governors, judges, and other high officials and their wives, together with committee men and women," her daughter, Mary Axelson, said. "[She and my father] were in frequent attendance at parties at the White House where Mrs. Roosevelt introduced my mother as "the best friend I have in Oklahoma."

After retirement, the couple continued to divide their time between Sapulpa and Florida. Oklahoma loved Myrtle and all the work she had done for her city and state. Two of the state honors that pleased both her and her husband were the honorary LLD. degree for her service to the state from Oklahoma A&M College in Stillwater, Oklahoma, now Oklahoma State University, and being named honorary colonel of the Oklahoma National Guard by Governor W. H. Murray.

While Myrtle was happy in her social and political work, she was also fulfilled in her home life and the raising of her three daughters, Myrtle A. MacKay, Mary McDougal Axelson, and Miss Violet A. McDougal. She continued to wield her influence and was pleased when Oklahoma Governor John C. Walton named Violet, her youngest daughter, Oklahoma's first poet laureate in 1923.

When Myrtle died at her home in Coral Gables, Florida, on Wednesday, July 25, 1956, two weeks before her ninetieth birthday, she could rest easy. She had done more than most people do to justify their existence. She had founded or led more than forty civic groups and helped institute legislation not only for the city of Sapulpa, but for Oklahoma and the nation. Her father would have been proud.

Augusta Corson Metcalfe

(1881–1971)

PRAIRIE PAINTER

❝My time has been crowded with work, but now I can devote some
to my painting and I wish to ask you for the description of the truce
of "Iron Jacket" at Antelope Hills," Augusta Corson Metcalfe wrote in a
letter to Joseph Thoburn, on April 6, 1911, from Durham, Oklahoma.
"Which side of the hills was it on and in which position? I can get many
views, but I would like the right one."

Many critics thought Augusta Corson Metcalfe put too many details
into her paintings, but that detail is exactly what made her paintings
famous and valuable. Metcalfe lived the paintings and drawings she produced. Though she had no formal art training, she became known as the
Sage Brush Artist and the Grandma Moses of the West. She called herself "a memory artist." Her work has been exhibited in galleries across
the country and museums hold special exhibits of her work. Using pen
and ink, watercolors, and oils, Metcalfe captured a side of prairie life as
she experienced it and recorded moments in western Oklahoma history
as she saw it. Because of her special eye for detail, later generations enjoy
the same experiences.

Augusta Isabella Corson was born on November 10, 1881, near
Vermillion, Kansas. Her parents were Edward G. and Mary Davidson
Corson. Her father had been born in Pennsylvania in 1838. "'Pa,' as
we children called him, joined the Northern Army almost at the start of
the Rebellion," Metcalfe said in an interview with Melvin Harrel. "He
was discharged after a short training and only one skirmish because of
ill health." Metcalfe's mother was born in Philadelphia. Mary married

Augusta Corson Metcalfe Courtesy of the Augusta Metcalfe Museum and Break O'Day Farm

Edward there and Augusta's brothers and sister were born there before they headed west.

At age five, Augusta and her parents, along with her two brothers, Howard and Edward, and her sister, Janet, came to "No Man's Land," an area in the panhandle of what is now Oklahoma, from Kansas. The first house they lived in was a ten-by-twelve-foot shack. This was common among homesteaders, who would later build sod houses after they got used to the land. The Corson family also later built a sod house, a three-room structure the family lived in for six years.

Their first foray into the area was filled with new adventures, but not all of the family appreciated them. Janet got married and Edward went back to Kansas. This left Augusta with the chore of riding and bringing in the cows by herself. She didn't mind though. She loved being on a horse. She had her collie, Don, and her horse, Dick, to keep her company, so she did her chores happily, except when it was time for her schooling.

"The next year I had it hard," Augusta said in an interview late in life. "I had to study—do lessons. I would have much rather herd cattle. But Mother being a school teacher in Philadelphia, became a very good teacher and gave me a better education than most prairie children received."

In Augusta's spare time, she continued to spend her time outdoors and in the evening she would draw. She would fish, ride, and when available would scratch pictures into the soft sandstone rocks where she kept an eye on her cattle. Her favorite subjects were horses. As a matter of fact, her first picture, done at age four, was of horses. She couldn't get the legs right, but she practiced and practiced and practiced, until she did.

In the fall of 1893, the family moved farther south and began homesteading 640 acres at the mouth of Turkey Creek along the Washita River, six miles east of the Texas border. The homestead was located in Roger Mills County, near present day Durham, Oklahoma. The trip there had been another adventure. The South Canadian River was roaring due to recent rain. To cross it would be dangerous. After camping a few days, they decided to forge ahead.

"I was sitting on the seat with Mother and Howard, with Yip [one of her new dogs] on my lap." Metcalfe said. "A lot of things got wet. I still have a few of the valentines Aunt Belle had sent us from Philadelphia and they have the brand of that Canadian flood on them—river mud."

They settled on their claim and had their house built before the cold arrived. A neighbor helped them build a fireplace, and that was a blessing to the family when winter came full force. The family hadn't been on the homestead too long before there were rumors of an Indian uprising. Some settlers packed up and moved over into Texas, but Metcalfe's family stayed put. Soldiers came shortly thereafter and said they were able to calm the Indians down. The Metcalfe family was safe.

In 1894, Howard, Augusta's eldest brother, became sick, and after going to Kansas City to see a specialist, passed away. She was closest to Howard and took his death hard. Her younger brother, Edward, and his wife came from Missouri in 1895 and tried to make a go of it along the Washita, but after a year they went back to Missouri.

Augusta made many new friends in this area of the state when settlers started coming in to claim their land. Towns started springing up, with saloons, churches, and post offices. Mail was still a challenge, but when a neighbor went to town they picked up the mail of all their neighbors too. Through all this time, Augusta was soaking up the things happening in her environment and drawing them. Drawing was second nature to her. It was something she did all the time.

"[Drawing and painting] was just something I used to 'kill time with' as I was home most of the time," Augusta said in the interview. "I didn't go places like folks do now. I used to send drawings to my Uncle George in San Francisco, and he would sometimes tell me what was wrong with them. He also sent me drawing paper, pencils, etc. I wanted to try color, but it was his idea to learn to draw before using colors."

The life of a pioneer, young or old, was not easy. Augusta and her mother raised turkey and chickens, churned butter, grew and tended a garden, picked berries and did the washing and mending for the entire family. Neighbors got together frequently, either dropping by or at the dances and picnics organized for everyone.

Augusta's father started showing signs of mental decline in the early 1900s. He wandered off from the homestead, wouldn't do chores, and showed a propensity for violence. When he did work on the homestead, the results could be disastrous—like the day he set a woodpile on fire, causing a huge prairie fire. Augusta took over his chores, and in the evenings worked on her drawing and painting for an hour or so before going to bed.

For several years, Augusta's mother had been submitting stories to magazines for publication as a way to supplement the family income. On a number of occasions, Augusta submitted illustrations for these stories. At one point, Augusta even had a book of her drawings printed, titled *Wild Animals I Have Known.*

As Pa's condition continued to worsen, his behavior became more erratic. In 1902, after a very violent episode, he left his family and ended up at the National Military Home in Leavenworth, Kansas. He died the following year there. The cause of death was stated as epilepsy brought on by a head wound or some disease he picked up during his time in the army.

Neighbors including James Metcalf came to the ladies' aid after Augusta's father died. This assistance grew into a romance and Augusta married James in December 1905. The following August, the couple had a son whom Augusta named Howard after her beloved brother.

James turned out to be a frequent gambler and was good for nothing but trouble. Whether Augusta knew his faults before their marriage is unknown, but in any case, the marriage did not last long. There were reports that the friction between Augusta's mother and James is what drove him away. Whatever happened, he left his mark on Augusta in more ways than one.

First, he left a stack of wood from a building project in a dangerous place. Augusta's mother fell over it, broke her hip, and was never the same. Second, he left Augusta with their son, who hadn't even turned two. This left Augusta with not only an ailing aging mother, but a baby, all the homestead chores, and taking care of the family's homestead business as well.

Her only written comments about James were in response to a Kansas woman's letter wanting to know Augusta's opinion of him. She wrote: " . . . there is no good in him. I would not believe him on oath. He wanted to get possession of my horses and they would have been turned into money to gamble on. He never bought a single thing for the boy. Wherever he went he made mischief. I have farmed now for four years, besides being housekeeper as my mother is an invalid (having broken a hip through his means)."

After her husband's departure, Augusta decided a change was in order. She added an "e" to her married last name, gritted her teeth, and became her own woman. She got up early, did all the chores, and at the end of the day, though totally exhausted, she sat down and faithfully worked on her art. She was determined to survive without father, brother, or husband. She would never marry again.

Being now the sole support for her family, Augusta set to work making money any way she could. In 1909, 1910, and 1911 she entered her artwork in the Oklahoma State Fair and won a total of six awards. This drew the attention of Joseph B. Thoburn, Oklahoma historian, and T. C. Moore, Roger Mills County School Superindentent. She came to elicit the opinion of Thoburn, who hoped he could help sell her work through minor exhibits. She was not shy in self promotion, and worked tirelessly at it. In one instance, she drew the favor of Thomas Edison, the great inventor. She used his commendations in her ads and writings in an attempt to get recognition for her work.

On September 13, 1912, Augusta's divorce was final. That part of her life was behind her. She adored and doted on her son. He would become her reason for going on and her support as she grew older.

As time went on, Augusta had all but given up hope of achieving fame and prosperity through her artwork. Nobody wanted to buy her pictures, so she threw herself full time into running and managing the ranch and farm. She learned about gas leases and mortgages, and used these options to supplement the homestead operations when needed.

She continued to do her artwork, but for her own personal pleasure. She took the occasional commission and continued to draw and do watercolors on postcards, stationery, and envelopes as she had for so many years. Augusta exchanged her skill in training horses for illustrations. The Beery Company used her illustrations in advertisements while Augusta got mail order lessons on training horses.

As her mother's health continued to decline, Augusta took over the writing of her mother's journal. Her mother had kept track of weather conditions, crops they had raised, animals they had on the property, and people who came and went. In early 1918, her mother updated her will, leaving all of her property to Augusta. Augusta continued keeping close track of World War I as more and more men from her area were being called away to fight. To help the war effort, she sent a painting to the Red Cross organization in an effort to help them benefit in their efforts.

By November, news came of the war's end. The year had been fraught with floods, measles, and the latest illness, Spanish flu. While everyone else was out celebrating the end of the world, Augusta isolated her family from everyone for fear exposing her family. Her biggest concern was that her mother would not survive the illness as so many had already died.

In her journal entries, Augusta talks about her painting, music, and farm and ranch chores. The Corson Metcalfe's had survived 1918 and 1919. On February 22, 1920, however, Augusta's mother, her rock, partner, and friend, passed away.

The 1920s brought a lot of change to Augusta's world. She voted for the first time, saw airplanes in the skies, and enjoyed owning a car. Howard turned eighteen during that decade, and mother and son named their homestead Break O'Day Farm.

As Howard got older, he was able to take on extra farm work. This helped Augusta greatly as it freed up more time for her to work on her paintings. Her work won ribbons at fairs in Perryton and Abilene, Texas. The work the Metcalfes put into the farm made it successful in the twenties and into the thirties. While many people were losing their farms, the Metcalfes persevered. During the Great Depression and the Dust Bowl, though times were difficult, they persisted. The pair was nothing if not flexible in their endeavors. They had the ranch, farm, a dairy, bees for honey, chickens and turkeys, Howard's small car tinkering business, and Augusta's card and stationery illustrating, which continued to bring in money. It was enough.

Howard said later in life that it was the dairy that kept them afloat during the financial hard times. During those years, they watched many of their neighbors leave the area for a much brighter future in California.

In 1940, Howard joined the military by choice. While the president had enacted a peacetime draft, Howard was exempt because he was an only son. He was assigned to the Army Corp and after travels through the Pacific Islands, New Caledonia, and Biak, an island off Australia's coast, he ended up in the Pacific Islands working on airplanes.

While Howard was gone, Augusta had the help of a neighbor and his family. Augusta worked the farm and ranch as she had always done and continued with her letter writing and her artwork. Howard received many letters from Augusta while serving overseas. She would write and illustrate them, telling him about what was happening on the farm and her opinions of the war.

When Howard was discharged from the military in 1945, he married a local girl, Helen Klingman. After a California honeymoon, they returned to Durham and the farm to settle down. Howard built his new wife and his mother a new two-story home. Howard and Helen would live in the second story while Augusta lived in the bottom.

With the return of her son, Augusta had added time to work on her art. A few years later, the Durham Willing Workers, a social and service club in the area, sponsored an exhibit of Augusta's work. This brought it to the attention of one Daisy Dunn, who became Augusta's self-appointed, unofficial agent. She knew all the right people and began dragging Augusta to one social event after another, showing off her drawings and paintings.

In 1947, Augusta was featured as a guest on a WKY television show in Oklahoma City, the Edd Lemons *Saturday Farm Fair.* This created more exposure for her work and was the beginning of the recognition Augusta had sought when she was younger. Two years later, writer Roy Stewart wrote about her and her artwork for the *Daily Oklahoman.* Nan Sheets, artist and Oklahoma City Art Center director, read the article and decided to hold an exhibit of Augusta's paintings at the Oklahoma Art Center in June. This created a buzz, which started a tumbleweed effect. *Life* magazine published an article about her in July 1950 and the Philbrook Museum in Tulsa wrote that they would be exhibiting one of Augusta's paintings. She was invited to enter paintings in the Philbrook's Oklahoma Annual the following year, and Director Robert M. Church said he would keep her in mind for exhibitions in the future.

Augusta's course was set now as the famed artist she had wanted to become. Commissions came regularly, and she was making money with them. At the same time, she was traveling around with her paintings for exhibitions and enjoying the attention she was receiving. With her increased income she began traveling to places she had wanted to see, and visited Texas, Kansas, and Mexico.

She was honored when Nolan McWhirter, curator for the No Man's Land Historical Museum in the Oklahoma panhandle, asked if she would be interested in exhibiting her work there. She jumped at the chance. Many more such opportunities opened up for her.

In 1955 a biographical sketch Melvin Harrel wrote about her appeared in the *Chronicles of Oklahoma*. That same year she received $250 for two paintings she had given as gifts to Governor Raymond Cary. He wrote to thank her, and told her one would hang in his office and the other in his reception area.

In 1957, her work began to be shown on the New York art scene. Richard V. Goetz of the Goetz Studio wrote that he had sent two of her paintings to New York City to be included in an exhibit at the Grand Central Art Gallery. This got Augusta's work on the list of many gallery directors, who began requesting to see her artwork. This was a double honor as number one, she was a woman, and number two, she was self-taught. The art world at the time was a bit snobbish, and exhibitions by unschooled artists were unheard of. On top of that, she didn't go out and sketch, as many other artists did. She remembered and created her art pieces from memory.

"She never had an art lesson and she never copied. Sometimes someone would insist she copy certain pictures and she would do it, but she didn't like to," her son, Howard, said in an interview after his mother passed away. "They were all originals. She seldom if ever took a sketch of anything—she remembered what it looked like when she got home maybe six months or a year or two later and tell you."

Augusta's success was reflected in more than numerous exhibitions and increased income: The Durham Willing Workers commissioned a portrait of Augusta to be painted by John Shelby Metcalf of Oklahoma City. It was accepted by the Oklahoma Historical Society in Roger Mills County and hangs in the Cheyenne Black Kettle Museum. Also, a documentary was made about her life. Meanwhile, her work continued to be hung in places of prominence like museums and the New York Biltmore Hotel. In 1968 she was inducted into the Oklahoma Hall of Fame for her lifetime achievement. Augusta was eighty-seven.

Her eyesight had always been an issue, but she continued to do her artwork. No doubt the time of day in which she had found time to draw and paint and the conditions under which she strained contributed to the deterioration of her sight.

"She would work and would draw at night. She didn't do it for profit. She enjoyed it and she kept on many a night. It may have been 11:00 p.m. and she was still doing something by a coal-oil lantern. She painted until two years before she died," Howard continued in the interview. "After she had cataract operations on both her eyes, her vision was bad. . . . She couldn't see right and she knew it."

Besides the disappointing eyesight that followed her surgery, there was an even more troubling development. Augusta began to lose her mental acuity.

In the late sixties, she had to give up painting. Helen and Howard found her one day in her studio splattering paint all over a canvas not knowing why or what she was doing. On another occasion, she tried to start a fire on the wooden staircase to cook breakfast. She was admitted to All Faith Nursing Home in Sayre, Oklahoma, in January 1971. She died there five months later.

Forty years after her death, Augusta's pictures live on in museums, private collections, and at the homestead, which was turned into a museum of her life and works. When one looks at her pictures, they tell a story and give a historically accurate portrait of life on the prairie. In them we see her memories, as vivid in color as a writer's would be with words. "She made pictures of everything that she knew, and she didn't make pictures when she didn't know."

DOROTHY K. BARRACK
PRESSLER MORGAN

(1896–1978)
PIONEERING PILOT

At the beginning of the twentieth century, aviation was coming into its own. The Wright Brothers had made history with their flying machine in 1903, and other men had made strides in the aviation field in the following years. While women may have been fascinated, not many were up to the challenge. There were a few, however, who threw caution to the clouds, and Dorothy Pressler Morgan was one.

"I really couldn't say how I got interested in flying," she said in an article in the *Oklahoma Times* in 1969, "but at the time I didn't have much else to do. A friend thought I'd like to learn to fly—and I did."

Dorothy Barrack Pressler Morgan was born on May 19, 1896, in Parkersburg, West Virginia. She came to Oklahoma in the 1920s with her husband, Howard Pressler, and they settled in Perry, Oklahoma. While Howard worked away from home doing field work for the Magnolia Petroleum Company, Dorothy filled her time playing bridge.

For the adventurous Dorothy, card games grew old quickly. For a change of pace, she decided to take flying lessons. Each week, she drove from Perry to Oklahoma City to attend flying class at the Graham Flying School, where classes cost $21 an hour, which in the twenties was a lot of money. She started in 1929. Her first plane was a single-engine, open-cockpit OX5 American Eagle. In the early days of flying, it wasn't glamorous or all fun.

"It was lots of hard, hard work with no limits on hours," Dorothy said in an interview for the *Sunday Oklahoman* in 1963. "You'd have to

Dorothy Morgan (right) with Amelia Earhart (center) and an unidentified woman
Courtesy of the Research Division of the Oklahoma Historical Society, Oklahoma City

love what you were doing to spend long hours in the open, in wind and dust, to clear runways and do all kinds of manual labor."

When Dorothy started flying, flying schools used open-cockpit planes for instruction. They had no instrumentation or navigational equipment. One learned to fly with a compass, good eyesight, and lots of luck.

"I have always thought it was a good thing I didn't know much about flying when I got started. I didn't know enough to be afraid. We just killed people off right and left. You couldn't open a paper without seeing where someone got cracked up."

Fear never fazed Dorothy. She was doing what she loved, and nothing was going to stop her. Curiosity had gotten her started, but she had always been interested in transportation, and how things moved. Her father had been a railroad engineer, and she guessed that's where her interest really started.

She had twelve hours and thirty-five minutes fly time when she had her first solo flight in April 1929. "That was not too few or too many for a woman." There was a lot of debate among the boys about whether Dorothy could or would fly, but she had the last laugh. Dorothy described her experience in a 1977 interview with Mary Roberts for the Oklahoma Historical Society.

"I worried them considerably on my first solo. I was learning to fly off the Southwest Twenty-Ninth Street Airport just off May Avenue. They had just one runway that could be called a runway, and of course it was not paved. We had to come in over Wilson and Company, and over high lines where the stockyards were. I took off and went around the field to land. When I did, I pulled the knob off the stick, and it fell on the floor. That did excite me considerably because I really didn't know what to do."

There was a slot in the floor where the controls were, and she was afraid the knob had fallen in there. "I did remember that they said if you run into difficulty trying to land, go around the field again until you collect your wits and come in. I went around and came back in again, and by that time I had my fingers in the top of the stick and I could hold on to it real good. I landed and bounced a little, of course, and came on in. Clint Johnson was one of the Graham Flying Service executives. I told him, 'Well, I got down all right.' They told me afterwards that he bit the stem off his pipe, he was so worried. I said, 'Yes, he was worried about his ten-thousand-dollar airplane, not me.'"

Dorothy got her pilot's license in 1931. It was a big day for not only her, but women in general. There was only one other female pilot flying in Oklahoma, May Haizlip. Her husband, Jim, was a flight instructor in Norman and taught her to fly. May was a race pilot. She and Dorothy became good friends. Through the years and their careers, they kept in touch.

It was around this time that Curtis Wright, a large national firm, bought out and then expanded the Graham Flying School. They put in a large hangar and brought in a lot of planes. Dorothy went around trying to get students for the school. She especially wanted to recruit women, but mostly just men signed up, and that disappointed her. "I was preaching to every woman I could talk to, but there was a real block there," Dorothy continued in her interview with Roberts. "You came into the difficulty of their husbands didn't want them to fly, their fathers didn't want them to fly, nobody wanted them to fly, but me."

Even for the women who were encouraged to fly, money was an obstacle. It was expensive. Dorothy finally went to work for Curtis Wright as a clerk so she could continue her flying lessons. "I went to work and turned my check over to them to pay for my flying."

During the Depression and when money was hard to come by, Dorothy did some acrobatic flying. She taught herself to do flying tricks by watching "the boys." The first stunts she did were barnstorming and doing loops over towns like Lawton, Enid, Chandler, and Geary. These tricks were meant to attract attention so the men, Ted Colbert and Clyde Knuckles, could go in and carry passengers. They'd pick up passengers, take them up over town, and then bring them back for five dollars. Business was pretty good as people were fascinated with flying.

Dorothy finally joined the Curtiss-Wright Flying Circus and debuted in a Commandaire airplane. She was considered Oklahoma City's best stunt flyer and those who saw her perform agreed. Her performance included six loops, the roll, wingovers, and the spin of death. Her spin of death was what caught people's attention. She'd fly up to an altitude of two thousand feet, go into a tailspin, level off, cut the motor, and then finally land to the crowd's explosion of applause. Dorothy also entered air races and performed in air programs. That's how she met Wiley Post and Amelia Earhart.

"I knew her well," Dorothy said of Amelia. "She was a very nice person who never threw her weight around."

Wiley Post was a close friend of Dorothy's and considered her a capable pilot.

"One thing I always felt was a feather in my cap was when Wiley came back from his trip around the world. He had a Bird Airplane," Dorothy said in her interview with Roberts. "He came into the field where we were, on his way to his home in Maysville, Oklahoma. As was customary when you got a new airplane, you let your friends fly it—just test hop it around the field. Several of the boys flew the plane. When he got through with them, he asked if I wanted to go for a ride. He said, 'Go out and get in.' I thought he was going to take me for a hop. I got in, fastened down; he came back and showed me several things on the plane including something new called a starter. I waited for him to get in and he said, 'Well, go ahead.' I said, 'By myself?' His reply was, 'Of course. You can fly as well as those fellows can.'"

Dorothy had learned to fly by using her good judgment. Because flying was so new, she learned to fly like 'the boys' learned, through trial and error. On her first solo cross-country flight, she flew from Oklahoma City to Tulsa. At the time, they didn't file flight plans and didn't have charts; pilots just flew by what they knew of the land. Dorothy wasn't very worried. She had handled maps when she had worked for the Magnolia Petroleum Company Land Department.

On this particular day, she was flying a Challenger Fledgling and following a plane. The weather wasn't very good. They were supposed to land in Bristow and wait until the weather cleared before they continued on, but when the plane in front of Dorothy flew right into the clouds, she knew that wasn't for her. She didn't believe in flying into disorienting clouds, so she decided to turn around and go back to Oklahoma City.

"I, of course, got lost," Dorothy said in her interview. "Then I remembered that if you didn't know where you were, get low and follow a road out until you came to something you could recognize."

Dorothy did find her way to Bristow, and they finally all made it to Tulsa. After that, Dorothy flew cross country to Dallas; Wichita; Garden City, Kansas; and back to Oklahoma City.

In 1934, Dorothy received her transport pilot license. "I was thrilled to death," she remembered. In 1932, there were only five thousand licensed pilots in the United States and only twenty transport-rated women pilots. To get a transport license, pilots needed two hundred flying hours and had to take three tests. The first two tests were for private and limited commercial, which allowed pilots to transport passengers; another was for transport, which allowed pilots to transport anything their plane was big enough to carry. It was at this time that Dorothy developed a cataract in one eye. "I had to take a test every time I turned around so that I could prove I could fly with only one eye, like Wiley Post."

Dorothy was involved in only one air accident, and she wasn't even the pilot when the incident occurred. She and the pilot were taking pictures of oil wells for a client when they ran out of gas. They landed in a cornfield near Binger, where they got gas, but when they tried to take off, the plane flipped upside down. Dorothy was afraid of fire, as gas was leaking all over her pink dress and black stockings and shoes. People came and cut her out of her seatbelt. She fell out of the plane with a thud and banged up her thumb when the Fairchild camera she was holding fell and hit it. Despite the accident, Dorothy was determined to continue flying. She was one of a handful of women pilots, and she wanted to see more women become involved in flying. To do so meant she had to bring attention to what then was considered the sport of flying. Part of that job was to test planes and see what each new one could do and to set records if possible.

On August 4, 1931, Dorothy and Captain Bill Bleakley were assigned to test a new plane, the Curtiss-Wright Junior. Dorothy had been flying the open-cockpit, light plane, and they wanted to see how high an altitude the plane would reach. The record at the time for planes of that weight was around fifteen thousand feet.

"It was in August when we have buildups of clouds. We took off with full tanks, wearing heavy clothes, boots, and prepared for zero weather. The fur-lined flying suit I wore weighed more than I do," Dorothy said. "We flew and I took advantage of every cloud and the updrafts. I got boosted to 16,091 feet when I ran out of gas, which was supposed to be done. I started down and ran through two snowstorms at various altitudes, but came on in. As soon as we landed, they ran out and grabbed our wings to keep us from getting blown off the field.

"Bill had gotten the barograph from Fort Sill and the Federal Aeronautical Institute to monitor our flight. Unfortunately, the barograph uses India ink, which is based on water, and it froze. After the freezing point as we went up, it did not register and we had no verification. This made it unofficial and I never did try it again. I don't know whether I would have ever gotten that high again since it was the weather that boosted me."

Dorothy and others were clearing a path for women in aviation in the 1930s, partially through the efforts of the Ninety-Nines club. This international women pilots organization, which officially began in 1929, offered support for women pilots and worked to change legislation if needed so that aviation would be more accessible to women. Dorothy was a founding member of the group, one of the original "ninety-nine" charter members, though bad weather prevented her from attending a group meeting until 1939.

While Amelia Earhart was serving as president of the Ninety-Nines, Dorothy continued her membership, but was also on the board of directors and was secretary for the Oklahoma Aviation Service. She was a member of the Aviation Committee of Oklahoma City Chamber of Commerce, the National Aeronautical Association, the Betsy Ross Air Corps, and the Oklahoma City Altrusa Club.

In 1933 she became the nation's first woman municipal airport manager after she was appointed interim manager of the Oklahoma City Municipal Airport, which is now Will Rogers World Airport. Most people might believe that this was a cushy appointment, but it was not. It was a twenty-four-hour job, and Dorothy learned quickly that she could be called at any time of the day or night for anything. In October of that year, she was called in to manage her airport as the FBI escorted "Machine Gun" George Kelly and Kathryn Kelly through its corridors. They had been involved with four others in the kidnapping of Charles Urschel, an oilman and one of the richest men in Oklahoma City.

Dorothy also had to alert pilots of cows on the runway, and she was also called in frequently in the middle of the night to clear birds, particularly ducks, off the tarmac. She got pretty good with a shotgun.

Dorothy married her second husband, Merrill Morgan, in 1937. She'd met him years earlier while they were both taking flying lessons, though Dorothy soloed before he did. After their wedding they took a whistle-stop flying tour around the United States. Merrill worked for the Federal Aviation Agency. Dorothy loved flying, and flying with her husband was all the sweeter. But when Dorothy got pregnant, all that changed.

"They had a rule that if you were pregnant, you could not fly," Dorothy said. "They cancelled your license." For those women who did want children and wanted to fly, this was a double hardship. Dorothy was outraged. It took her a long time to get her license and it cost her a lot of money. She couldn't afford to take all those classes again. She spoke to the Ninety-Nines and the president of that organization, who backed Dorothy up. She told her to write down what she thought about the rule, and she said she would see if she couldn't get something done about it. The rule was in effect for two years, but finally the pilots associations got involved, took it up with Washington, and got the rule cancelled.

For Dorothy though, flying was out of the cards. Having her daughter, Sharon, was a factor, but so was her deteriorating eyesight. Even though she couldn't pilot a plane, she still continued to stay in the business. She got a job as secretary at Tinker Air Force Base.

During World War II, the couple moved temporarily to Houston, while Merrill trained the Air Transport Command to do instrument flying. The stay wasn't long, and they came back to Oklahoma City. Merrill died in 1955.

"I had to hurry and get back to work," Dorothy said in her recorded interview. She took a job at the Federal Aviation Administration herself until she retired in June of 1967.

When asked before her death about the changes she'd seen in aviation, she mentioned higher speeds and more reliable equipment. Dorothy knew pilots no longer had to fly by the seat of their pants, be their own weathermen, and that women made as many contributions to flight as men.

Dorothy passed away in Oklahoma City at St. Anthony's Hospital on January 31, 1978, after a long illness. In her obituary they called her a pioneer woman aviator. She became known nationwide in the 1930s as being one of only five women in the United States who held a transport pilot license.

She would have been pleased to know that in 1992 the Oklahoma Aviation and Space Hall of Fame honored her by giving her its Pioneer Award. She was a pioneer, the first female pilot in Oklahoma, and the first female in the United States to be rated as an airline transport pilot. And even though she was lesser known than Amelia Earhart, Dorothy Pressler Morgan cleared a path for all the women who fly today.

LUCILLE MULHALL

(1885–1940)

QUEEN OF COWGIRLS

Lucille Mulhall was known by many titles. When she rode out on Governor, her trick horse, during her father's shows, she was America's Greatest Horsewoman. When she rode wildly and roped steers in competition with the men, she was World's Champion Roper. When she rode in parades and opening ceremonies she was Queen of the Range. Crowds paid money to see her ride and cheered enthusiastically as she exhibited her skills. Cowboys respected her. The press loved her. Yet, when she was home, she was Lucille, America's First Cowgirl, who loved horses, roping, and ranch life.

Lucille Mulhall was born in St. Louis, Missouri, on October 21, 1885, to Zack and Agnes Mulhall. Her father was born Zachariah P. Vandeveer in 1847. His mother died when he was young and at the age of eight, in 1855, his father died of yellow fever. He was sent to live with his aunt and her husband, Mr. and Mrs. Joseph Mulhall, in St. Louis. While there are no records stating that he was adopted by the Mulhalls, Zack took the name of the couple who raised him. Another orphan came to live with the couple as well, Mary Agnes Locke. She was related to Joseph Mulhall. Mary Agnes, after receiving her college degree from Notre Dame in 1870, married Zack in 1875. They had eight children, but only two, Agnes and Lucille, survived to adulthood. Lucille also had two half-siblings, Charley and Mildred, son and daughter born to her father and his mistress, Georgia.

Lucille's father's early business consisted of contracting cattle shipments from the ranchers in Texas and Indian Territory for the Santa Fe Railroad. On one of the trips into the Territory, he found a piece of land

Lucille Mulhall Courtesy of the Research Division of the Oklahoma Historical Society, Oklahoma City

he wanted, so in true Mulhall style, when the land was opened for home-steading in the run of 1889, Zack Mulhall staked his claim. A year later he moved his family down to his eighty-two-thousand-acre ranch, forty miles north of Oklahoma City, and a fifteen-room house he had built for them. It was here that Lucille would become the horsewoman people across the world would come to know. She was only five.

Already at this young age, Lucille loved the ranch. Her family may have had an inkling of the horsewoman she would become when they sat two-year-old Lucy on a horse, and she cried when taken off. Now, the ranch offered her all kinds of time with horses. She spent most of her days outdoors, roping steers or riding horses, the wilder the better.

When her older brother, Logan, died of diphtheria in 1895, Lucille took his place in helping run the ranch. All the cowhands came to respect her skill and accepted her, as she could cut any cow from the herd as well as the next man. With all the work she was doing, she decided she wanted to have a ranch and cattle of her own. She begged her father for a herd and he told her she could have as many of the calves as she could catch and brand. He called a halt to her activities, however, when *all* the calves he started seeing had her brand on them.

It was around this same time that Lucille and her brother, Char-ley, became local celebrities—Lucille for her roping and Charley for his bucking bronc riding. They not only put on shows for the hands at their father's ranch, but were invited to Guthrie by the mayor to enter-tain his guests.

Lucille's mother had worried for her safety for a number of years. She didn't think a young girl should be out roping wild steers. Her worry increased tenfold when Lucille was hurt roping a steer and ended up bruised and in bed for a week nursing her injuries. Her mother wanted to send her off to St. Louis to boarding school. Her father stood up for her, and the crisis was momentarily averted when Lucille promised she wouldn't rope steers again. That promise was broken some months later when Lucille rode out and attempted to rope the largest steer on the ranch. Not only did the steer die, but so almost did Lucille. The matter was then settled. Lucille was packed up and shipped off to boarding school as soon as arrangements could be made.

The following year was not a happy time for her. The convent sisters wrote to her parents telling them that while Lucille's grades were good, she was homesick for the ranch. There seemed to be no amount of work or activity that could snap Lucille out of her malaise.

After getting that report, Lucille's parents decided perhaps schooling closer to home might be the best thing for her. They decided that in the fall, Lucille would attend St. Joseph's Convent School in Guthrie, Oklahoma. It was a boarding school, so she would stay at school through the week and come home to the ranch on the weekend. This suited Lucille just fine.

When Zack went to pick Lucille up in St. Louis to bring her home, he took a riding outfit he had commissioned for her. They also visited the fairgrounds there before heading back to Mulhall. While there the pair saw a horse, Governor, doing simple tricks. Lucille fell in love with him, so her father bought him for her. This horse would become as famous as Lucille and carried her to many events, showing off his skills as well as helping her with hers.

The Mulhall Ranch had many visitors through the years. Teddy Roosevelt, Will Rogers, and Tom Mix were only a few of the men to come through and stay awhile. The Mulhalls first met Teddy Roosevelt when he came to Oklahoma City for a reunion of his Rough Riders in 1900. The Colonel and the Mulhalls were asked to put on a show for the Rough Riders and they did. Roosevelt was especially taken with Lucille's horsemanship and her ability with a rope. Colonel Zack and Colonel Roosevelt hit it off, and Roosevelt was invited back to the Ranch.

One day, as the two of them stood watching Lucille rope and tie a large range steer, Roosevelt turned to Mulhall and smiled. "Zack, before that girl dies or gets married, or cuts up some other caper, you ought to put her on the stage and let the world see what she can do," Roosevelt said. "She's simply great!" And Roosevelt at that time should have known. He was a rancher himself in the Dakota Territory.

In later years, Zack would tell people that it was Roosevelt who gave him the idea for the show, when in truth, Mulhall had already started down the show path. Roosevelt just fed his ego and gave him the confidence to continue. When Theodore Roosevelt was elected president in 1904, Lucille, her father, and the show's band went to Washington and rode in Roosevelt's inaugural parade. Lucille's career and her popularity began a meteoric rise.

Will Rogers and Tom Mix got their start in shows on the Mulhall Ranch. Rogers and Lucille worked together, practicing their acts. Rogers showed Lucille his fancy tricks, and he was impressed with her roping and riding abilities.

In 1900, Colonel Zack took Lucille, her horse Governor, Rogers, Mix, Charley, the band, and several other ranch hands to the Louisiana Purchase Exposition in St. Louis to put on a Wild West Show. The show was a success and opened up opportunities for them to appear in exhibitions, contests, and shows.

"Lucille was just a little kid when we were in St. Louis that year, but she was running and riding, her ponytail all over the place and that was incidentally her start too," Rogers wrote in an article in the *Daily Oklahoman* on Sunday, October 11, 1931. "It was not only her start, but it was the direct start of what has since come to be known as the cowgirl. As Colonel Mulhall from that date drifted into the professional end of the contest and show business, Lucille gradually came to the front, and you can go tell the world that his youngest daughter was the first well-known cowgirl.

"She became a very expert roper and was the first girl that could rope and tie a steer, not only do it but do it in such a time that it would make a good roper hustle to beat her."

The troop traveled across the country showing what they could do. Charley was becoming known for his bucking animal riding, be it steers, wild horses, or anything else that could be caught and held until he could get on. Lucille was a draw because of her riding and roping abilities. Audiences may have been skeptical about Lucille's skills when the group arrived, but by the time they left, everyone respected her talents.

One such town was El Paso, Texas. No one believed Zack's comments that his daughter could rope and tie a steer, least of all the local saloon owner. He posted odds that not only could she *not* rope and tie, but that she couldn't even rope. Zack bet on Lucille at ten-to-one odds.

When she first rode out, she missed the steer's horns, but on the second round, she not only roped the steer, but she tied it. The crowd went crazy. Not only that, they stormed the field and started tearing off her clothes. In a world where men had always been at the top of the barn ladder, they didn't believe Lucille was a girl. Charlie rode out and rescued her while Colonel Zack collected ten thousand dollars off the whole affair.

Lest people think her horsemanship abilities made her any less a woman, it did not. Her schooling had trained her to be a lady, and she was a beautiful one at that. She could read, sing, sew, and write; after all, she had attended finishing school and could rub shoulders with any other debutante of that day, as she was a cultured young woman. She could hold her own in society. The only difference was that she could rope, throw, and tie a steer in twenty-eight and one-half seconds.

As one can imagine, injuries came with the riding, roping, and steer tying. Lucille had her share of mishaps. One year in St. Louis, Lucille broke her ankle while roping a steer in a steer-roping contest. On another occasion while putting Governor through his paces, as she reached down to pick up a handkerchief as part of a trick, she reached over too far, got stuck in the stirrup and Governor dragged her across the arena. While people ran to assist her, she shook off, caught up with Governor, remounted, and continued with the trick. The crowd saw her resilience and loved it.

Her father's legal problems followed the troop after he shot three men at the 1904 St. Louis World Fair, was charged with assault and intent to kill, and many years later was sued by the plaintiffs. While Lucille loved the contest and the roar of the crowd, those times cannot have been happy ones. In 1906, Mulhall shut the troop down. The Mulhalls went back to their ranch where they spent a year quietly recovering from the circuit they had been on.

In 1907, her father secured several contracts that would literally put Lucille on the stage, a vaudeville stage. Her brother, Charley, and several of the cowboys from the ranch appeared in the show. It was called "Lucille Mulhall and Her Ranch Boys." The *St. Louis Republic* was the first to announce the show.

> *Miss Lucille Mulhall of 4643 Washington Boulevard, fearless young horsewoman, well known throughout the United States because of her appearance in her father's Wild West shows in many cities, is to go into vaudeville.*
>
> *Her engagements will begin January 20 in the Orpheum in Kansas City, where her father has completed a contract for her appearance in a number of shows for the rest of the season. The vaudeville act will be modeled after the wild west shows in which she has taken part so often.*

The tour was composed of one- to two-week stands in towns such as Omaha, Minneapolis, Pittsburgh, Cleveland, Chicago, Memphis, Louisville, Cincinnati, Philadelphia, and Brooklyn. The Mulhalls' part of the show lasted about thirty minutes. A young man, Martin Van Bergen, who sang for the show, was paired with Lucille for the opening set. After the song, Lucille performed tricks and maneuvers with Governor and then riding stunts. The stages she performed on were not very large, so she rapidly learned how to get her horse to stop quickly, lest she be thrown off his back and the stage and be injured.

In late 1907, rumors began to circulate that Lucille had married Van Bergen. She denied this at first, but by 1908, while in Kansas, she announced in an interview that they had been married in Brooklyn, New York, on September 14, 1907.

The following year the couple had a son, William Logan Van Bergen. Lucille took off through 1908 and most of 1909 to be a wife and mother. It is reported that Lucille made an appearance at the 101 Ranch Rodeo in 1909. It isn't known whether that show is what sparked Lucille's ambitions to return to the show circuit or if that is what she had planned all along. What is known is that in the fall of that year, she left her son in the care of Van Bergen's parents, and the Mulhalls went on the road again, this time as Lucille Mulhall's Broncho Busting Company. Their first stop was in St. Joseph, Missouri, for the Horse and Interstate Livestock Show. Lucille, and Mildred did their horse and roping tricks, while Charley performed riding bucking broncos. Since Van Bergen is not mentioned in the act, it is likely he returned to vaudeville.

In the following year, Lucille's father put together one of the most ambitious shows to date. Besides starring Lucille, Mildred, and Charley doing their acts, he included several skits like the Pony Express and a stage coach hold-up. There were races, a trapeze act, tribal dances, and a Mexican bull fight. While there was a lot of excitement about the show, there was also a lot of controversy. The first was over the Mexican bull fight; the second over an accident that occurred in the stagecoach skit in which three female passengers, including Mildred, Lucille's sister, were injured; and the third over the way animals, particularly steers, were treated in such shows. Lucille was front and center in the steer incident.

The show had traveled to Chicago. Lucille was giving an exhibition of steer roping. A Chicago newspaper shared the story with those who were not able to attend.

Several hundred men, women, and children saw a badly fright-ened steer killed yesterday at the Coliseum by the woman roper, Lucille Mulhall. When the animal, struggling feebly as it was dragged about the ring by the young woman, gave a compulsive gasp and became unconscious, a cry of disgust and horror arose from the audience and a dozen cowboys rushed forward and dragged the carcass from the arena.

At that time, steers were roped around the neck. But after that things began to change. The Society for the Prevention of Cruelty to Animals stepped in, bringing charges against the Mulhalls and even though nothing much came out of the action except for some fines, the SPCA started getting legislation passed in states prohibiting steer roping.

In November of 1910, Lucille and Martin Van Bergen appeared one last time together in Arkansas. Not long afterward, perhaps reflecting how they had gone in different directions, they divorced.

Lucille had a difficult private life. Her life consisted of being on the road and pleasing her father. Lucille's father had not wanted her to marry. Being known as the "World's Greatest Horsewoman" had an image that demanded a certain reputation be lived up to like being tough and as rough as the west itself.

Financial woes soon caused the big show to disband. Lucille and Charley formed their own show, but eventually Charley went his own way. Lucille formed her own company, Lucille Mulhall and Company. She continued to perform not only in Wild West shows, but in theater settings as well. One week would find her in Montana, the next in Texas, Kansas, or Iowa.

Other cowgirls were entering the scene by 1915, and Lucille competed against them in the rodeos. She was still a draw, but her times were slowing down in competitions with other women. When she helped manage a stock show in Texas, Lucille got an idea that would still keep her involved in shows: She would become her own rodeo promoter. In addition to promoting rodeos, where other cowboys and cowgirls came to compete, Lucille performed at these events and gave exhibitions.

World War I bought a lull in performing in 1917 and 1918. Lucille continued to attend cattlemen's conventions, and at one of these she met and befriended Tom L. Burnett. He was a well-known Texas rancher who came from a family with oil money. The couple was married on April 14, 1919. Lucille got involved in rodeos again briefly. By April 1922, the couple was divorced, and Lucille headed back to Oklahoma and the Mulhall Ranch.

Lucille settled into life on the ranch with her parents. She didn't go back on the road or perform again. On January 30, 1931, her mother died of cancer, which had been diagnosed a year earlier. Her father, Zack Mulhall, died the same year, on September 19, at the ranch.

Mildred and Charley came back to the ranch to live with Lucille after their divorces. Lucille rode in parades, and Charley put on amateur rodeos at the ranch. In September 1940, Lucille rode as an honored guest in the Cherokee Strip Parade. It was held in Ponca City and was to celebrate the land run of 1893. The parade would be Lucille's last public appearance.

Two months after her fifty-fifth birthday, Lucille, her brother, and his new wife were coming home from a visit in Orlanda, Oklahoma, a town six miles from Mulhall, when their vehicle was struck by a truck. Lucille was killed a mile from her beloved ranch. The date was December 21, 1940. The *Daily Oklahoman* included an article about her funeral, and in it was a line that conveyed the irony of her death,

"As a cold rain whipped across the bleak eroded homestead that once measured its range in thousands of acres, Lucille Mulhall, the world's first and most famous cowgirl, was buried Thursday. . . . A machine killed Lucille Mulhall, but horses brought her to her final resting place."

Lucille was inducted into the Rodeo Hall of Fame in December 1975, the National Cowgirl Hall of Fame in 1977, and in April 1985, the

Eighty-Niner Celebration in Guthrie, Oklahoma, honored her by dedicating their all-day event to Lucille.

Today, when one speaks of cowgirls, Lucille's name is always brought into the conversation, as well it should be. She paved the way for women to compete and be known for their skills in the Western arena. Today's cowgirls know this. Lucille would be happy to know many still remember her for her horsewoman skills and abilities, and that she still lives in the hearts of many horsewomen and is known as a pioneer in their field.

ALICE MARY ROBERTSON

(1854–1931)
CONGRESSWOMAN

"I want that appointment," Alice Mary Robertson wrote to President Theodore Roosevelt in a letter dated December 24, 1901, "because I believe I am better fitted by training and experience to perform its duties than anyone else. The existing conditions in this Territory are so diverse and anomalous that no stranger can possibly do intelligent work without first giving much preparatory study to these conditions."

The job Robertson sought was "supervisor of schools in Indian Territory." In the early twentieth century, women weren't allowed and weren't supposed to be involved. However, with the tides of change sweeping not only Indian Territory, but the nation as well, women began working to anchor that change in their own lives. While Mary Alice Robertson was not a part of the suffrage movement and on occasion spoke out against it, she helped changed the perception of women in politics and made her mark in the politics of her day, not by radicalism or by proclaiming or playing the female card, but by being herself and voting her moral convictions.

Mary Alice Robertson was born in Indian Territory at the Tullahassee Mission on January 2, 1854, to William Schenck and Ann Eliza (Worcester) Robertson. The mission was located in Wagoner County near Muskogee. Her parents were both missionaries to the Creek Indians. Her mother had the distinction of being the daughter of Reverend Samuel A. Worcester. He was missionary to the Cherokees and spent time in a Georgia prison for his devotion to them. Alice's mother also was responsible for translating the Bible into the Creek language so the Creek people could read the Bible on their own.

MUSKOGEE
INDIAN TERRITORY
EUFAULA

TRAVELLING
L. F. Standiford
Photographer
ARTIST
Parsons, Kan.

McALESTER
INDIAN TERRITORY
VINITA

Alice Mary Robertson Courtesy of the Papers of the Robertson and Worcester Families 1815–1932, coll.
No. 1931.001, Department of Special Collections and University Archives, McFarlin Library, University of Tulsa

From an early age, Alice and her four siblings were taught and expected to live by the edicts of the Bible. "My parents were connected with an Indian boarding school at the time of my birth, and services were held in the assembly room of the school, so my church going began when I was three weeks old and has been continuous since," Alice said in an article for the *Muskogee Daily Phoenix* on Sunday, November 24, 1929.

When the Civil War started, the missionary family was driven from the Creek Nation. Their immediate escape was to Park Hill, a home given to Alice's grandfather by the Missions of the American Board. Even though her grandfather had died in 1859, it was still a gathering place for the family. Alice remembered seeing an aunt and uncle there when they arrived. None of the family stayed long, as tensions and mistrust grew and festered within the family group.

Alice had always lived among the Indians, but as her family traveled back east heading for their final destination, Wisconsin, where her father's parents were missionaries, she was introduced to the white man's world. As the family traveled by wagon, and night pressed upon them, the family grew tired and they stopped at the house of a white man who had a Cherokee wife. Alice's father didn't trust the man, but because they were hungry and tired decided not to press on.

Alice later wrote about what happened there in her personal family recollections: "In the early gray of the morning, when dawn was just beginning, I was awakened by the sound of voices, and listening intently, I heard the Cherokee woman begging her husband for my father's life. He was planning to call a posse of neighbors and hang father as a Yankee spy." Her father got up and sneaked away, securing a pass from General Price, who was camped not far away with his Confederate soldiers.

The family made it to Wisconsin where Alice attended school for a while. Later the family moved to Highland, Kansas, where she continued her studies. They returned to Tullahassee in 1866.

"Urgent calls came for the return of the missionaries to Indian Territory," Alice wrote in her papers, *Remembrances of Childhood.* "The Indian people were coming back from the exile from their refugee camps in Kansas, so in December 1866, two missionary families of us started from the old Iowa Mission near Highland, Kansas." As they traveled south, more wagons joined their party. Every morning, Alice's family said their prayers and didn't move on until that was done. The family also didn't travel on the Sabbath. It never failed that the missionaries always caught up with and passed the other travelers, who had to deal wagon wheels busting or horses sinking in mud or breaking their legs.

"They seemed to make no better time than we did, for we would pass them never later than Thursday in the week, and then they would come on and pass us again on Sunday. They did not seem impressed with our religious observances."

After they got back to Oklahoma, Alice didn't continue her formal education, but studied under her father for the next five years. In 1871, when Alice was only seventeen, she headed east once again. She entered Elmira College in New York where she studied history, civics, and English until 1873. Part of her civics classes included trips to Washington, DC, where she met many prominent political figures including President and Mrs. Grant. That year, she left college to take a job as clerk in the Office of Indian Affairs in Washington so she could provide for an education for her sister. It was through her family's missionary work and her political connections that she secured the clerking job and became the first female to hold that position. While in Washington, she continued her education, learning shorthand and taking domestic science classes. For a while, she returned to Indian Territory to help her mother with mission work, but was called back to Washington and then transferred to Carlisle, Pennsylvania, to serve as secretary to Captain Pratt of Carlisle Indian School. She saw this as an opportunity "to fit herself for service among the Indians."

Even though she was in the East, Native Americans, especially the children, were never far from her thoughts. In 1880, when a fire destroyed over half of the Tullahassee mission, Robertson worked to find a place for twenty-five students and raised funds to secure their relocation.

When her father died in 1882, she was recalled to Indian Territory and new responsibilities. Besides taking over her father's work, she helped with her mother's as well, since Mrs. Robertson's health was failing. Using her newly acquired education, she set about helping those in her sphere of influence. Her education in domestic science and her experience with politics and world affairs had prepared her well.

She accepted a teaching position in Okmulgee at the Creek School. While there it became apparent that funds for education were low. The Civil War, an internal war in 1881, and subsequent reprisals known as the Green Peach War, put an increasing demand on the Creek coffers. But Robertson set to work raising money in the East and raised enough money to establish Nuyaka Mission in Okmulgee.

Robertson was also instrumental in starting the University of Tulsa. In 1885 she was sent to Muskogee to run the Presbyterian School of Girls, a boarding school for Creek, Cherokee, Choctaw, Chickasaw, and Seminole girls. That school became the Henry Kendall College and moved to Tulsa, later being renamed the University of Tulsa.

Alice spent fifteen years at the school, holding various positions, even professor at one point. Because she always had an interest in education, she was honored to receive an honorary Master of Arts degree from Elmira College in 1886.

As the nineteenth century was closing and the twentieth was on the horizon, Alice sought new ways to work for the peoples of Indian Territory. She attended conferences and seminars whose main topics were Indian Reform. At an annual Friends of the Indian conference at Lake Mohonk in New York, Alice met Board of Indian Commission members and individuals interested in the true welfare of the

Five Civilized Tribes in Indian Territory. In 1892 Alice was to speak at this conference. Among the attendees that heard her was Theodore Roosevelt. Then a civil service commissioner for President Benjamin Harrison's administration, he listened to Robertson's speech with much interest. He was impressed with Robertson's conservative views and agreed with her argument over the advantages and disadvantages of government versus mission schools. After her speech, Roosevelt couldn't wait to meet Robertson, and he told her, "Your views on education are mine also."

Seven years after their initial meeting, seeking an appointment as supervisor of schools in the Indian Territory, she wrote a letter to then New York Governor Theodore Roosevelt, asking for his help with a recommendation. The two remained close and sealed their relationship when Alice helped recruit soldiers for Roosevelt's Rough Riders in the United States war with Spain in 1898. Now, the tables were turned, and she was asking for his help.

"According to Oliver Wendell Holmes the training of a child should begin a hundred years before his birth. My training in Indian work began thirty years before I was born, when in 1825, my grandfather, Samuel A. Worcester went to labor among the Cherokees at Missionary Ridge," Alice wrote. She then went on to list her qualifications and told the Governor why she was the best person for the job.

She finished with, "I know I am 'capable and competent' and that I have had 'experience in educational work.' The only required qualification upon which I feel doubtful is as to whether I am sufficiently 'discreet.' I could try to be, and I believe I could be, 'Discreet' in this connection I understand to be the ability to see everything and say nothing except in reports to my superior officers.

"At present I am professor of history in Henry Kendall College, but I covet the larger opportunity at the crisis in the affairs of the people with whom we have so long been identified."

Roosevelt wrote a glowing recommendation letter, and Robertson received the position. Her duties for the school involved appointing teachers, school visitations, auditing school accounts, preparing statistics, and writing up quarterly and annual reports for review by the federal government. These responsibilities required that she travel throughout Creek County in her horse and buggy. There were no hotels at the time as the county was sparsely populated, so she sought refuge in the homes of Indian friends who were always glad to see her.

She enjoyed what she was doing and felt she was making a difference. However, as her ailing mother aged, she knew she couldn't continue to travel around the Territory and still care for her. She again wrote to Roosevelt, who was now president. She wanted him to appoint her postmistress of the Muskogee Post Office.

This wasn't a job women sought or held. Positions as postmaster were usually a political gift given in return for help with political campaigns. Robertson, being a woman, had no political clout, but Roosevelt did not always follow tradition. In December 1904 he sent his nomination to the Senate. Alice became postmaster of the Muskogee Post Office in 1905. She was the first woman in the United States to hold that first-class post-office position.

The new appointment allowed Robertson to save some money, and in 1910 she purchased a fifty-five-acre farm west of Muskogee on Agency Hill. She built a large home for the time and named it Sawokla, which is Creek for "gathering place." It had large fireplaces and porches that overlooked the woods around the property. Her home would become instrumental in some very important meetings held for veterans and by the Oklahoma Press Association.

Her farm was a working farm. Robertson not only raised vegetables, Guernsey and Jersey cows, but Duroc Jersey pigs, and leghorn hens. At first it was a truck-farm operation, but she expanded that into a cafeteria business in Muskogee. The cows supplied milk and butter, while her chickens provided eggs. Her garden brought fresh produce to the tables. Her products supplied the cafeteria and gave working girls a place where they could find good, wholesome food. In the beginning, the cafeteria was just for women, but later expanded to serve a general clientele. When she left the post office in 1912, she turned her attentions to her successful farm.

Robertson was already well known in the area because of her family's work and her political connections, but she was about to become even more well known for her charity, kindness, and the hospitality she gave to World War I soldiers passing through the area. Miss Alice, as she became known, went to meet the trainloads of soldiers as they passed through Muskogee on their way to training camps in Texas. At first, it was small groups to whom she took doughnuts, sandwiches, and coffee, but the groups grew. As they did, she obtained an empty railroad car where she set up a canteen for the passing soldiers. All the southwestern training camps knew that when stopping through Muskogee you were guaranteed a free hot meal, and if you needed a place to stay the night, you were always welcome at Miss Alice's farm, Sawokla. Meeting the trains and feeding the troops became of upmost importance to her. In the end, she fed thousands of soldiers and their families if need be, as they passed through Muskogee.

Robertson, at times, seemed an enigma. She didn't agree with Roosevelt that Oklahoma and Indian Territory should become joined as a state, yet she petitioned for government rights for the peoples of the area. She opposed women's suffrage, and even joined the National Association Opposed to Women's Suffrage and served as its vice president, yet in 1920, she announced her intent to run for a congressional seat. The anti-suffragettes believed that women should not be involved in politics because they felt it was, number one, a dirty business, and number two, that it would "diminish women's established sphere in the home, where they upheld the virtues of American society."

Robertson didn't fit any of the molds that society dictated for women: She had never married, didn't have any children of her own, and didn't have a family sphere to influence in the traditional sense. She had raised a daughter, Suzanne, handed over to her by the girl's dying mother. Alice promised she would raise the girl and did a good job. Suzanne later married one of the richest men in Tulsa.

Unlike the men who ran for political office, traveling around the country and giving speeches, Robertson fought for her congressional seat with the help of the newspaper. She had done well by advertising her cafeteria in the paper, so she would use that mode of communication for her election campaign. Through a series of ads in the *Muskogee Daily Phoenix,* she wrote to residents in her district telling them what she stood for, what she wanted to do, and what she thought needed to be changed. She also made it clear that her own hard work and initiative, not her political affiliation, had made her a success. She would continue that same work ethic in Washington.

Robertson was well known in the community for her patriotism and for her public service, especially her support of women and soldiers. This reputation and her unorthodox campaign strategy helped her win the election, making her only the second woman in history to be elected to the House of Representatives. On June 20, 1921, she became the first woman to preside over the House of Representatives. Women thought she would vote and defend their interests; men, especially veterans, believed she would be a positive vote for them no matter what bill came across her desk. They were wrong.

Robertson was raised to believe that hard work gave people confidence and improved society in general. She disapproved of handouts and fought against legislation that provided financial assistance. She even opposed popular bills, such as the Soldiers Bonus Bill for veterans and the Maternity Bill for women. Her votes on these bills garnered a lot of negative attention, but she didn't care. She had to vote her conscience.

She interpreted these bills as making people dependent on the government, rather than truly helping them. In her term she did not support the League of Nations. She supported a bill to protect tariffs but would not support other parts of the bill and was opposed to the Sheppard-Towner Maternity and Infancy Bill because she felt it would diminish American liberty, which she felt was her responsibility to protect.

She wanted to explain why she was against the bills, feeling she was mostly misquoted by the press for her stands, but she didn't get many opportunities to do so. Her own League of Women Voters in Muskogee wouldn't even meet with her when they came to Washington and called her a "traitor to her own sex." They even planned to find another woman to run against her in 1922.

Robertson won the primary again in that year, but lost the election to W. W. Hastings. She had lost the soldiers' vote because she opposed the Bonus Bill and lost the women's vote because of her antifeminist position. She returned to Muskogee after her defeat and ironically enough became the director of the Muskogee Veterans' Hospital in May 1923.

She was a member of the Daughters of the American Revolution and gained their support through the years. In her last years, she worked for the Oklahoma Historical Society compiling her family's history and getting notes and artifacts ready to be donated to the McFarlin Library of the University of Tulsa, for Oklahoma posterity.

Robertson issued one last printed statement on March 8, 1931, from Muskogee General Hospital for the *Muskogee Daily Phoenix*.

For some time I have been suffering from a sore mouth caused by a friction of a dental plate that should have been changed. On Tuesday, February 10th, my dentist to whom I had gone to insisted on an immediate consultation. Cancer of the lower jaw necessitated a speedy and painful operation. Wednesday and Thursday I spent in arranging affairs, Friday I came to the

Hospital and Saturday went safely through the ordeal of having a cancer burnt out by electricity. For days I was only half conscious of what was going on, but careful record was kept of letters, telegrams, gifts flowers, etc.

The surgery left Robertson unable to speak and was obviously not successful. She wrote she was to remain in the hospital indefinitely, which wasn't long. Robertson passed away three months later on July 1, 1931.

Even though she served only two years in the House, she left a legacy—not one of passing popular bills, but one she would describe as giving every American the chance to live independently. That's how she lived, true to herself, not to a party or affiliation, but to acting for what she thought was good for each individual. She was a caring, honest, and loyal person, and that is what she was most proud of and how she wanted the people of Creek County to remember her.

KATE GALT ZANEIS

(1887–1973)
COLLEGE PRESIDENT

66 I think I'll succeed or fail in this job on my own merits, without the fact that I'm the only woman to head a state college," Kate Galt Zaneis said in an interview for the *Daily Oklahoman* in 1935. The first woman to be named president of Southeastern State Teachers College in southeastern Oklahoma—and any college in the nation for that matter—went on to state, "That is of course the way it ought to be in everything—but, unfortunately, it isn't. There is no reason why women shouldn't have had a fair proportion of college presidencies before, but it just wasn't 'traditional.'"

Miss Kate, as everyone around the Ardmore and Durant, Oklahoma, area called her, was born to teach and, in particular, to teach leaders about how to instruct children, a task whose importance she recognized, since children grow up to be the ones building new communities. She achieved much in the area of education and could have achieved even more at Southeastern State if a group of men hadn't stood in her way and ultimately stopped her efforts. She was a strong woman though, and like other women with backbone, she picked herself up, brushed herself off, and became an example for other women of the state and across the country.

Kathrine Benton Galt was born on February 17, 1887, in Springplace, Georgia, to James Edward and Miriam Otis Galt. While the couple had gone to Oklahoma in Indian Territory days and maintained a residence in Ardmore, Oklahoma, Miriam always went back to Georgia to deliver her babies. Afterward, when mother and child were well enough to travel, they would return to Ardmore to continue with their lives. Kate was the fourth of eight children, four boys and four girls.

Kate Galt Zaneis Courtesy of the Research Division of the Oklahoma Historical Society, Oklahoma City

James Edward, Kate's father, was a carpenter and a contractor, and he ran a boardinghouse. Kate's mother was a former teacher, so the Galt children began their education around their huge kitchen table under the tutelage of their mother.

Kate was an excellent student and at an early age showed promise that she might be an educator herself. A favorite childhood game was to gather the neighborhood children and play "school," Kate of course, would always be the teacher. If someone else took an interest in instructing the children, she lost interest.

When she entered public school, she was the brightest and most involved one there. In high school she participated in drama and debate, served as librarian because the school couldn't afford one, was editor of the Ardmore High School newspaper, *The Criterion,* tutored younger students, and worked as a substitute teacher on occasion.

She graduated from Ardmore High School in 1907 at the top of her class. So impressed was the superintendent of schools, Dr. Charles Evans, that he gave her a special gift for her academic achievements, a job teaching in his school district without requiring a college degree. "Teachers are born and not made," Dr. Evans told the commencement audience, "and Kate was most assuredly one of those born to lead."

After teaching for six years for Dr. Evans, in 1913 Galt met and married an oil field worker, Herma Prince Zaneis. She had first met him in 1910 when he came to her father's boardinghouse for meals. He was a fireman then, working for the Rock Island Railroad. Three years later he started working in the oil fields. After the couple married, Kate gave up teaching, and they moved to Wirt, Oklahoma. The marriage lasted only two years. There were no children from the union, so after the divorce, Kate returned to Ardmore and became not only principal of Lincoln Ward School, but teacher and janitor as well.

As much as Kate loved school when she was growing up, as an adult she loved it even more. Education became her whole life. She ate, lived, slept, and breathed education. She loved her students and would do anything to help them succeed.

In 1915, she became superintendent of Rexroat Consolidated School and Lone Grove High School. Two years later she was invited to Southeastern State Teachers College to teach over the summer. This was common practice at the time. By inviting superintendents from schools in the area, colleges found they could attract students from those schools in the following years.

Kate was impressed with Southeastern and the work it was doing to further education. She knew this was the college she wanted to attend to get her bachelor's degree. At Southeastern she saw what was possible with education, and she knew she had to get politically active to make those possibilities a reality for her state. Oklahoma's educational system needed reform, and that is the platform she ran on in her bid to become superintendent of public schools. She wanted to take the eighty one-room schools in Carter County and consolidate them into fewer, larger schools. In 1920 she won her bid to oversee the school system of Carter County. All was not blissful when consolidation began to take place. Parents objected to having their children sent away from a place near their home on a school bus. The consolidation of a school near Wilson and Healdton, in fact, angered the public so badly that the sheriff had to station deputies outside Kate's home night and day to protect her. She also insisted that schools for black children in Carter County be upgraded and consolidated as well. This didn't set well with the public either.

Consolidation was just one of the goals Kate adopted during her tenure. As an appointee to the Citizens Committee on Education for Remedial Legislation, she and four other members traveled to different states to learn about other school systems, to see if successful innovations made by schools elsewhere could be adopted by Oklahoma's system. They then reported to and sent their recommendations to the

Oklahoma legislature. Kate initiated the school lunch program, which fed many hungry students during the Depression and beyond.

In 1922 she decided it was time to go to college. She resigned her superintendent position and enrolled in Southeastern, where she studied for four years, graduating with honors in 1926. Only then did she return to a teaching position in Carter County. Life was busy and at times difficult for Kate during those four years. She worked in the Oklahoma Education Association, became a member of the County Excise Board, and stayed active in her church teaching Sunday School and attending Methodist church conventions. Her father had been born into a Baptist family, but when he married Kate's mother, he changed his affiliation to hers and became a Methodist. The family remained so. He passed away in February 1924.

All was not sadness at his passing, however, as during this time Kate and her mother met a young woman by the name of Pearl Brent. Pearl was eager to learn, and Kate was more than happy to assist anyone with a desire for education. She and her mother hired "Miss Pearl," as they came to call her, as housekeeper, and she became a part of the family, taking care of them, cleaning, cooking, washing their clothes, even nursing Kate's mother when she became ill. Miss Pearl was the one who kept things running smoothly. She didn't mind though. It is said she worshipped Kate and her mother.

After graduation and her return to teaching, Kate served the children of the county until 1934 when a practice so upset her that it pulled her back into politics and a role that would change her and the state forever.

While the Depression was affecting everyone's lives, perhaps education was feeling its effects the most. Since money was scarce, school districts were issuing pay warrants instead of checks to teachers. These were basically "promises to pay" from the government. No one would accept these warrants except banks, and they charged teachers a fee for taking them. The fee caused a teacher's pay to be even lower. After Kate received a pay warrant, and learning of the "fee" banks were charging, she took to the streets of Ardmore and denounced the practice. She told an enthusiastic four hundred listeners that it was time people supported a candidate for governor who supported education and wouldn't let this type of fiasco go on. She suggested that E. W. Marland was the man for the job.

One of Marland's campaign workers had heard Zaneis's speech and told him about it. Marland contacted Kate and requested she join his campaign. She agreed, became his campaign manager for the county, and traveled throughout the state not only making speeches on his behalf, but traveling with the candidate himself.

After Marland won the election, he appointed Kate to the state board of education and his citizens' committee on education. While serving on the committee, Kate helped write House Bill 212 and got it before the 1935 Oklahoma Legislature. The bill did three things with its passage: First, it created a school financing method that brought money to the educational system. Second, it did away with pay warrants for teachers. Third, it established a sabbatical leave with pay so teachers could take advanced studies to get an advanced degree.

At the same time Zaneis was fighting for reform, she began studies for her master's degree at Oklahoma A&M, now Oklahoma State University. She was set to graduate in May of that year when a couple of developments suggested that more than a degree was on the horizon. At the beginning of the month, much to everyone's surprise, Zaneis resigned her position on the board of education. On May 11, Governor Marland commented to the *Daily Oklahoman* that he would like "to see a woman head one of our normal schools." Since Marland controlled the state board of education with appointments, it was a foregone conclusion that he already had someone in mind.

Then, just two days before she graduated, Governor Marland named Zaneis the new president of Southeastern State Teachers College, the first woman president of a four-year state college in the nation. She was just forty-one.

Zaneis, of course, saw this as a boost to women's rights and a wonderful opportunity. She didn't see the downside: Powerful players in education and government as well as some private citizens were opposed to her appointment, some because they opposed this kind of progress and a few because they wanted the position themselves. Zaneis had suddenly made enemies and would be working under a microscope.

With her appointment coming virtually on her graduation, she couldn't immediately get away, so she called Southeastern State's head of the Department of Education, Dr. Everett Fixley, and asked him to take over for her until she could get there. When she did arrive, a big gala was held for her. Governor Marland and his wife attended, as well as five hundred others.

"I come to Durant to accept the greatest task I have ever undertaken," she said to the crowd of supporters, "Southeastern is not a new love; it is an old love which I have come back to renew."

At first, Zaneis had the support of most of the community. After all, she knew almost everyone in the Ardmore and Durant area. She had grown up there. Her family had lived there. She, her mother, and Miss Pearl still lived in Ardmore. But some of the changes she made eroded that support.

Her first order of business was to name the dean of students. Going against popular opinion, she named Everett Fixley as dean over a local favorite, R. R. Tompkins. Rumors spread about Fixley's reputation, that he had attended wife-swapping parties and had met his wife at one in San Antonio. Zaneis wasn't interested in rumors. She wanted the most qualified person for the job and felt Fixley was it. He stayed.

Her next order of business was to replace professors who didn't have college degrees with those who did. She fired those who had worked for the college for a number of years and hired teachers from not only out of town but out of state as well. Two of the teachers replaced were well liked around Durant, so this was another black mark against her in the community.

Keeping with her change and betterment attitude, she ordered the campus to be cleaned up. She also established regular morning meetings with faculty at seven o'clock and required a dress code. While the faculty was still smarting about the dress code, she informed them that there were inequities in the pay scale which she aimed to correct. Under her tenure, all pay scales would begin at $150. For the female teachers of the group, that was great news. It was a pay raise, and for some quite a substantial pay raise, as some were only receiving from $50 to $100.

Zaneis explained the highest salary would be $180 for women and men. This meant a pay cut for the men. They were not happy. Immediately the men began to voice their disapproval, but Zaneis had made a decision, and she was sticking to it. Professor T. A. Houston would have been wise to keep his mouth shut. When he continued to complain about his salary being cut back to $225 in a late night phone call to Zaneis, she responded the next morning by informing everyone of her mistake. After careful review of the budget, Professor Houston's salary would now be $180 instead of the amount stated earlier in the week.

After her faculty and budget were taken care of, she continued her work on improvements to the campus and to reducing the debt the school had incurred under the former president's tenure. First, she contacted the Oklahoma legislature for emergency appropriations, and second, she applied for assistance from President Franklin D. Roosevelt's New Deal Plan. That application netted the college thirty thousand dollars in Public Works Administration monies. This paid for new concrete floors in the science building, new furniture, cabinets, and a fresh coat of paint, to name just a few things.

Zaneis would next tackle enrollment. In January 1935 enrollment at the school was at an all-time low. The president knew this would have to change if the college was to improve, and so she began what many called a recruitment blitz. She had the college's newspaper sent to local schools and recent graduates. She sent her professors out into the community to visit local schools to answer questions or otherwise inform prospective students about the college. She herself visited local schools. She brought cultural programs to the college that featured well-known personalities and special performers. She also invited state superintendents from other states to come and teach summer programs and set aside time to celebrate religious holidays. By the end of her first year, enrollment had increased by 33 percent.

Some of Zaneis's programs were not well received by the community. When the Frazer-James Dance Troupe appeared in December 1936, some frowned on their skimpy costumes. It was reported that Zaneis's own mother got up and left in the middle of a performance. However, Zaneis made the community proud and garnered back some good will when she arranged for Eleanor Roosevelt, first lady of the United States, to speak on Senior Day in May 1937. It was too late though. The term of her presidency was nearing an end.

As enrollment increased, so did the need for student accommodations. Students were being put up in attics, cellars, bed-and-breakfasts, tourist cabins, and on one occasion even in a tent city that Zaneis had approved for the young men until other accommodations could be arranged. Zaneis thought the solution would be to construct a women's dormitory and men's dormitory, and set about getting it done. The town didn't like the idea because they thought it would take business away from them, but Zaneis saw it as bringing more business to the town. She had requested $350,000 for the projects, and because of her persuasiveness, the legislation approved her measure.

Zaneis would not see the dorms built under her tenure. The state board of education called her in on the morning of May 22 and asked her to resign. When she asked them on what grounds and they did not and could not give her a reason, she refused. Later that day, she was sent word that she was fired. Because the board never came out and said exactly what Zaneis was being dismissed for, rumors started to circulate, not only among the town, but on the front page of newspaper. Some said it was because of the dorm issues, her plan to name the architect and oversee the use of the money herself. Others said it was because of the way she dismissed the professors when she first came into the job and the way she dealt with her teachers, cutting the male members' salaries, and requiring the early-morning meetings. Still others thought she had angered the board with her decorating and remodeling when she first came into office and with her regular teas and receptions. One article mentioned her cultural programs, while others discussed the enemies she had made with her decisions. But probably the one that was the closest to the truth is that she was fired because she was a woman.

"I am only one of hundreds of southeastern Oklahoma citizens who asked the State Board of Education to replace the woman college president," Claude C. Hatchett, a powerful Democrat and past president of the University of Oklahoma Board of Regents said in a public statement. "We feel her appointment here was a serious mistake. We have no real prejudice against Mrs. Zaneis, but we want a real man to head our college."

Even though she had made many profitable and useful changes to Southeastern, in the end it boiled down to her being dismissed, according to reports because of politics and the fact that she was a woman, meaning she did things and was going to do things men didn't approve of.

After she left Southeastern, she, her mother, and Miss Pearl moved to Oklahoma City where she worked at the Oklahoma State Capitol. For the next twenty-five years she continued to improve and make changes to the education system of Oklahoma. She served as director of education at the State Department of Public Safety, director of the Recording Division of the State Board of Public Welfare, and for the Public Relations

Division, Oklahoma Emergency Relief Board under the Department of Public Welfare.

In 1943 her mother passed away. She had had a prolonged illness, but Miss Pearl saw to her welfare. Zaneis retired in 1963. Miss Pearl passed away in early 1973 while she was recovering in the hospital from an illness after she fell and hit her head. Zaneis became despondent after Pearl's death and passed away herself on Sunday, September 9, 1973.

In retrospect, Zaneis was a woman ahead of her time. While she loved teaching, the problems she saw in education demanded to be fixed. Zaneis knew she was the woman to fix them. She faced many injustices, but she never let obstacles slow her down or stop her in her goal of improving Oklahoma's educational system. She was truly "Oklahoma's first lady of education."

BIBLIOGRAPHY

Catherine "Kate" Ann Barnard

Barnard, Catherine. Personal Correspondence. R. L. Williams Collection. Oklahoma Historical Society, Oklahoma City.

Burke, Bob, and Carlille, Glenda. *Kate Barnard: Oklahoma's Good Angel.* Edmond: University of Central Oklahoma Press, 2001.

Daily Oklahoman (Oklahoma City). "Barnard Gift Will Be Taken." February 27, 1930.

———. "Kate Barnard to Be Honored." February 25, 1930.

———. "Kate Barnard: Unsung Heroine." February 23, 1941.

———. "Orphan's Home to Be Investigated." March 13, 1914.

Edmondson, Linda, and Larason, Margaret. "Kate Barnard: The Story of a Woman Politician." *Chronicles of Oklahoma* 78 (Summer 2000): 160.

Federal Writer's Project. "Kate Barnard." Oklahoma Historical Society, Oklahoma City.

FS Barde Collection. Oklahoma Historical Society, Oklahoma City.

Huson, Hobart. "Oklahoma's Juvenile Court Law Most Effective of All." *Daily Oklahoman* (Oklahoma City), January 28, 1912.

Jesse J. Dunn Collection. Oklahoma Historical Society, Oklahoma City.

Musselwhite, Lynn. *One Woman's Political Journey: Kate Barnard and Social Reform 1875-1930.* Norman: University of Oklahoma Press, 2003.

New York Times. "Miss Kate, Livest Wire in Prison Reform Visits Us." December 8, 1912.

Ropp, Mrs. "Human Ideals in State Government," *The Survey Magazine* 23 (October 1909–March 1910), 16.

Schrems, Suzanne H. *Who's Rocking the Cradle?* Norman, OK: Horse Creek Publications, 2004.

St. Louis Post Dispatch. "Barnard and 'Bill' Murray Clash Again." March 17, 1915.

———. "'Grafters After Me,' Says Kate Barnard: Oklahoma's Guardian Angel Hits Foes Appeals to Legislature for Hearing." February 16, 1913.

St. Louis Republic. "'Oklahoma Kate' Warns Her Enemies She'll Be Ready for Next Campaign." February 16, 1913.

Sturm's Oklahoma Magazine (Tulsa, Indian Territory). "Oklahoma's Child Labor Laws," February 1, 1908, 42.

Weekly Chieftan (Vinita, Oklahoma). "Kate Barnard," April 29, 1910, 8.

Alice Brown Davis

Chronicles of Oklahoma. "Unveiling of the Sculptured Bronze of Alice Brown Davis, Chieftain of the Seminoles, Oklahoma Pavilion, New York World's Fair, June 12, 1964." Vol. 43 (1965), 94.

Cornelius, Frankie. "America's First Woman Chief." *Daily Oklahoman* (Oklahoma City), August 22, 1922.

Davis, Alice Brown Archives. Oklahoma City, Oklahoma Historical Society Library.

Foreman, Carolyn Thomas. "Chief Alice Brown Davis of the Seminole Nation." In *Indian Women Chiefs,* 62–67. Muskogee, OK: 1954.

Harris, Phil. "Fair to Call Attention to Area History." *Muskogee Sunday Phoenix,* sec. 4, June 7, 1964.

Hill, Rudolph N. "Seminole's Woman Chief." *Orbit Magazine,* April 14, 1974, 4.

Morris, Lerona Rosamond. *Oklahoma: Yesterday, Today, and Tomorrow.* Guthrie, Oklahoma: Co-Operative Publishing, December 1930.

Trimble, Vance H. *Alice & J.F.B.* Wilmington, DE: Market Tech Books, 2006.

Tushka Homan. "Mrs. Alice Brown Davis." July 30, 1935, Vertical File, Section X, Biographies. Oklahoma Historical Society Library Archives, Oklahoma City, Oklahoma.

Twin Territories Magazine. "Alice Brown Davis, First Seminole Chieftainess." Vertical Files, Research Division, Oklahoma History Center Archives, Oklahoma City, Oklahoma. p.16.

Waldowski, Paula. *Alice Brown Davis: A Leader of Her People.* March 20, 2010. Website of the Seminole Nation I.T. http://www.seminolenation-indianterritory.org/alice_brown_davis.htm.

Angie Debo

Blackburn, Bob L. "Oklahoma Historians Hall of Fame—Angie Debo." *Chronicles of Oklahoma* 72 (1994): 456–459.

Coffey, Ivey. "Indian History's Unfinished Chapter." *Oklahoma's Orbit,* November 21, 1971, 15.

Debo, Angie. Personal Letters. Oklahoma Historical Society, Oklahoma City.

———. "The Site of the Battle of Round Mountain, 1861." *Chronicles of Oklahoma* 27 (1949): 187–206.

Leckie, Shirley A. *Angie Debo: Pioneering Historian.* Norman: University of Oklahoma Press, 2000.

Loughlin, Patricia Erin. *Assuming Indian Voices.* Oklahoma City: Oklahoma Historical Society, 2000.

———. "Angie Debo: To Discover the Truth and Publish It." In *Hidden Treasures of the American West,* 69–109. New Mexico: University of New Mexico Press, 2005.

McIntosh, Kenneth. "Geronimo's Friend: Angie Debo and the New History." *Chronicles of Oklahoma* 66 (Summer 1988): 164–177.

Rachel Caroline Eaton

Bass, Althea, "A Cherokee Daughter of Mount Holyoke." Oklahoma City: Oklahoma Historical Society, 1937.

Berry, Christina. "Rachel Caroline Eaton—Cherokee Woman, Historian, and Educator." The All Things Cherokee website, www.allthingscherokee.com/ articles_culture_people_010201.html.

Eaton, Rachel Caroline. *John Ross and the Cherokee Indians.* Menasha, WI: George Banta Publishing, 1914.

———. "The Legend of the Battle of Claremore Mound, Oklahoma." In *The Traditional Background of the Indians.* General Federations of Women's Clubs, October 1930.

Fite, Mrs. R.L. *Historical Statement.* An Illustrated Souvenir Catalog of the Cherokee National Female Seminary, Tahlequah, Indian Territory, 1850–1906. E97.6 .C35 C45. Oklahoma History Center Archives, Oklahoma City, Oklahoma.

———. Historical Statement on the Cherokee. Oklahoma Historical Society, Oklahoma City.

Foreman, Carolyn Thomas. *Park Hill.* Muskogee, OK: The Star Printery, 1948.

Mihesuah, Devon A. *Cultivating the Rosebuds.* Champaign: University of Illinois Press, 1998.

Price, Warren C. "Removal of the Indians From Southeast a Major Tragedy." Ragland Collection. Oklahoma Historical Society, Oklahoma City.

Wright, Muriel, H. "Rachel Caroline Eaton." *Chronicles of Oklahoma* 16 (December 1938): 510.

"Tahlequah and Park Hill Area." Ragland Collection, 82.100, Box 23, Folder 8, Oklahoma Historical Society, Oklahoma City, Oklahoma.

Elva Shartel Ferguson

Carlile, Glenda. "Holiday on the Plains." *Oklahoma Today* 47, no. 5 (Nov.– Dec.1997):23.

Carter, Edward L. "Mrs. Tom B. Ferguson: Pioneer Woman Editor." In *The Story of Oklahoma Newspapers,* 105. Oklahoma City: Oklahoma Press Association, 1984.

Daily Oklahoman (Oklahoma City). "Mrs. Ferguson State Mother." April 30, 1946, 5.

Ferguson, Mrs. Tom B. *They Carried The Torch*. Kansas City: Burton Publishing Company, 1937.

———. "An Eighty-Niner and Ninety-Twoer Speaks." In *Oklahoma the Beautiful Land*. Oklahoma City: 1889ER Society, 1943.

———. "Mrs. Ferguson Writes About Topics of Days Back in Gay Nineties." *Daily Oklahoman* (Oklahoma City), November 13, 1932. Section C, 6.

———. "The Story of Oklahoma's Pioneer Newspapers." *Daily Oklahoman* (Oklahoma City), November 27, 1932. Section C, 7.

———. "The Story of Oklahoma's Pioneer Newspapers." *Daily Oklahoman* (Oklahoma City), December 11, 1932. Section C, 7.

———. "Statesmen With Courage to Say 'No' Were Needed Back in the Early Days." *Daily Oklahoman* (Oklahoma City), December 18, 1962. Section C, 7.

Hoxie, Mary Alice. "A Pioneer Woman of Oklahoma." Federal Writers' Project. Oklahoma History Center, Oklahoma City.

Morgan, Anne Hodges. "Picture of a Pioneer Town," In *Oklahoma Memories,* 113. Norman: University of Oklahoma Press, 1981.

Moudry, Frank. *Watonga 1892–1992*. December 1991, 45–47. Oklahoma History Center, Oklahoma City.

Patrick, Imogene. "'Sob Sisters?' Not Pioneer Lady Editors!" *Daily Oklahoman* (Oklahoma City), March 10, 1946, Section A, 18.

Rice, Darrell. "Watonga Post Office." In *Their Story: A Pioneer Days Album of the Blaine County Area,* 55. Oklahoma City: Heritage Book Committee, 1977.

Shaw, Ellen. *This Old House in Watonga*. Norman, OK: Recollections Press, 1989.

———. "T.B. Ferguson Home." In *A Centennial History of the Watonga Area: 1892-1992,* 379. Watonga, OK: Watonga Centennial History Committee, 1999

Annette Ross Hume

Chronicles of Oklahoma. "Annette Ross Hume." 11, no. 3 (September 1933): 1004-1005.

Daily Oklahoman (Oklahoma City). "Federation Formed in Spring of 1898 By Club Delegates." March 1, 1953, Section C, 4.

Hume, Annette Ross. Personal Letters. Annette Ross Hume Collection, Oklahoma Historical Society, Oklahoma City.

———. Personal Letters, Oklahoma City, Oklahoma, Oklahoma Historical Society, Oklahoma City, James Thoburn Collection, 86.01, Box 7, File Folder 11.

———. "An Historical Sketch," The Federation of Women's Clubs of Indian Territory 1898–1908." Oklahoma City, OK: Oklahoma State Federation of Women's Clubs.

———. "The Welfare of the Child." *Oklahoma State Federation News,* 1915, 3:7.

Hume, Robert Deniston. "He Traces His Descendants to Adam." *San Francisco Chronicle,* April 21, 1901, 26.

Lovett, John R. and Southwell, Kristina L. *Life at the Kiowa, Comanche, and Wichita Agency.* Norman: University of Oklahoma Press, 2010.

Myrtle Archer McDougal

Associated Press. "Two Women in Race For Democrat Committee Job." *Daily Oklahoman* (Oklahoma City), March 2, 1928, 1.

Associated Press. "Women to Play Prominent Part in Campaign." *Daily Oklahoman* (Oklahoma City), July 11, 1920, Section D, 9.

Axelson, Mary Carmack McDougal. *Thirteenth Child: The Story of D.A. McDougal.* Oklahoma City: Oklahoma Historical Society, 1966.

Hoder-Salmon, Marilyn. "Myrtle Archer McDougal: Leader of Oklahoma's 'Timid Sisters.'" *Chronicles of Oklahoma* 60, no.3 (1982): 332.

Jackson, Pauline P. "Life and Society in Sapulpa." *Chronicles of Oklahoma* 43 (1965): 297.

Johnson, Edith. "Success As an Organizer Gives Woman High Place." *Daily Oklahoman* (Oklahoma City), September 28, 1919, Section C, 7.

Leonard, John William. *Who's Who of America 1914-1915.* New York: American Commonwealth Company, 1914.

Oklahoma State Federation of Women's Clubs Yearbook 1909-1910.

Oklahoma State Federation of Women's Clubs Yearbook 1908-1913.

Augusta Corson Metcalfe

Harrel, Melvin. "My Life in the Indian Territory of Oklahoma: The Life of Augusta Corson Metcalfe." *Chronicles of Oklahoma* 33 (Spring 1955): pages 49–62.

Kelley, Suzzanne. "Augusta I.C. Metcalfe: 'Prairie Painter' of Memory Art." Thesis, University of Central Oklahoma, 2003.

Metcalfe, Augusta. Personal Letters. Oklahoma Historical Society Library Archives, Oklahoma City.

Olds, Fred. "Interview with Howard Metcalfe at Augusta Metcalfe's House." Oklahoma Historical Society Archives, Oklahoma City.

Stewart, Roy P. "Sagebrush Painter." *Daily Oklahoman* (Oklahoma City), April 10, 1949, 10-11.

Thoburn Collection. Oklahoma Historical Society Library Archives, Oklahoma City.

Warner, Elaine. "Augusta Corson Metcalfe." *Oklahoma Living.* March 2007, 29-30.

Dorothy K. Barrack Pressler Morgan

Betsy Ross Corps News. "Dorothy Pressler." May 1932, 6.

Claypool, Dorothy. "City Woman Is Marking Her 34th Year in Aviation," *Sunday Oklahoman* (Oklahoma City), January 27, 1963, Section C, 2.

"History of the Ninety-Nines, Inc." Archives, 99s Museum of Women Pilots, Oklahoma City.

Hodgman, Ann and Djabbaroff, Rudy. *Skystars.* Harrisonburg, VA: RR Donnelley and Sons, 1981.

Holden, Henry M. and Griffith, Lori. *Ladybirds:The Untold Story of Women Pilots in America.* Mount Freedom, NJ: Black Hawk Publishing Company, 1991.

Jessen, Gene Nora. "Women with Wings Meet Dorothy Morgan." *Western Flyer.* November 1974, 6.

———. "The Ninety Nines, 1929-1979." In *The Ninety-Nines: Yesterday-Today-Tomorrow.* 10–21. Paducah, KY: Turner Publishing Company, 1996.

Journal Record (Oklahoma City). "Aviation, Space Hall of Fame Honors Cooper, Inductees." November 11, 1992, 2.

Kansas City Journal Post. "Noted Women Fliers of Middle West Here for Betsy Ross Corps Rally." April 8, 1932.

Morgan, Dorothy. Personal Letters, from American Eagle, May 27, 1930.

———. Personal Letters, from Oklahoma City, dated October 2, 1950.

Oklahoma City Times. "Dorothy Morgan." February 1, 1978, 27.

Ostrand, Phil Van. "Early Woman Aviator Still Spry at 73." *Oklahoma City Times,* May 23, 1969, 7.

Owens, Violet. "Echo 1 Brings Echo of Past." *Beacon,* November 1960.

Roberts, Mary B. "Dorothy Morgan." Living Legends Oral History Collection. June 9, 1977. Oklahoma Historical Society, Oklahoma City.

Lucille Mulhall

Carlile, Glenda. "Lucille Mulhall—America's First Cowgirl." In *Buckskin, Calico and Lace: Oklahoma Territorial Women,* 129–142. Stillwater, OK: New Forums Press, 2008.

Daily Oklahoman (Oklahoma City). "Lucille Mulhall, World Famous Cowgirl and One-Time Toast of Royalty, Dies in Car Crash." December 23, 1940.

Guthrie Daily Leader. "Live Stock Convention." February 10, 1903, 5.

———. Society Page. February 27, 1903, 5.

"History of Mulhall." 83.213, Box 1, Folder 1. Oklahoma Historical Society Library Archives, Oklahoma City.

Mulhall Enterprise. "Three Shot by Mulhall," June 24, 1904.

Olds, Fred. "The Story of Lucille." *The War Chief: Official Publication of the Indian Territory Posse of Oklahoma Westerners* 8, no. 3 (Dec. 1974): 2–11.

Oral history given by Effie Strothman, *Oral History Tape #83.027,* February 7, 1983. 83.213.1. Oklahoma Historical Society Library, Oklahoma City, Oklahoma.

Rogers, Will. "Death of Mulhall Sends Wills Thoughts to Days When He got Show Bug." *Daily Oklahoman* (Oklahoma City), October 11, 1931, 23.

Stanbury, Kathryn B. *Lucille Mulhall: Her Family, Her Life, Her Times.* Mulhall, OK: K.B. Stansbury, 1985.

Tompkins Collection Scrapbooks 6, 7, and 9. Tompkins Exhibit No. 2. Oklahoma Historical Society Archives, Oklahoma City.

Alice Mary Robertson

Alice Robertson Collection. Oklahoma Historical Society, Oklahoma City. "The Honorable Alice M. Robertson." Biographical Sketches. Oklahoma Historical Society, Oklahoma City. "Miss Alice Mary Robertson," Biographies. Oklahoma Historical Society, Oklahoma City.

Clarke, James Vernol. "Presbyterian Woman in Congress," *New Era Magazine.* January 1921, 20-21.

Collins, Reba and Burke, Bob. *Alice Robertson, Congresswoman From Oklahoma.* Oklahoma Statesmen Series, Vol. VI, University of Central Oklahoma Press, Edmond, Oklahoma, 2001.

Cowgill, Elizabeth King. "Interesting Women of the Southwest: Alice M. Robertson-Second Congresswoman." *Holland's Magazine,* February 1921, 18.

Foreman, Grant. "The Honorable Alice M. Robertson." *Chronicles of Oklahoma* 10, no. 1 (March 1932): 13.

———. "The Lady From Oklahoma," *The Independent,* March 26, 1921.

James, Louise B. "Alice Mary Robertson-Anti-Feminist Congresswoman." *Chronicles of Oklahoma* 55 (Winter 1977-1978): 454–462.

Morgan, Tom P. "Miss Alice of Muskogee." *The Ladies Home Journal,* March 1921, 21.

Morris, Cheryl. "Alice M. Robertson: Friend or Foe of the American Soldier." *Journal of the West* (April 1973): 307–316.

Muskogee Times Democrat. "Our Postmaster Back from St. Loo." October 8, 1906.

Robertson, A. Augusta. "Alice Mary Robertson of Oklahoma." A. Augusta Robertson Moore Collection, 82.84, Box 1, Folder 2. Oklahoma City, Oklahoma: Oklahoma Historical Society, Oklahoma City.

Robertson, Alice. "Christmastime in Indian Territory." *Oklahoma Today* 32 (Winter 1981): 10.

———. "Miss Alice Has Big Time," *Muskogee Daily Phoenix,* November 24, 1929.

———. *Muskogee Daily News,* Miss Alice Says, 1925.

———. Personal Correspondence. Oklahoma Historical Society, Oklahoma City.

———. "Remembrances of Childhood: 1859–1867." Alice Robertson Papers. Oklahoma Historical Society, Oklahoma City.

———. "The Sheppard-Towner Bill." Congressional Record, Sixty-Seventh Congress, November 19, 1921.

———. "Title to Lands Within Pueblo Indian Land Grants," Congressional Record, Sixty-Seventh Congress, March 4, 1923.

Schrems, Suzanne H., *Who's Rocking the Cradle?* Norman, OK: Horse Creek Publications, 2004.

Stanley, Ruth Moore. "Alice M. Robertson, Oklahoma's First Congresswoman." *Chronicles of Oklahoma* 45 (1967): 2.

Spaulding, Joe Powell. "The Life of Mary Alice Robertson." PhD diss., University of Oklahoma, 1959.

The Literary Digest. "A Woman Who Got Into Congress Through the Want-Ad Columns." December 4, 1920, 56.

Kate Galt Zaneis

Beach, Linda Arlene. *Kate Galt Zaneis: First Lady of Education in Oklahoma."* Thesis, Southeastern Oklahoma State University, 1976.

Daily Oklahoman (Oklahoma City). "Durant Will Honor Mrs. Kate Zaneis." May 19, 1935, Section C, 10.

———. "Enrollment at Southeastern Is Expected to Reach 1200." June 7, 1936, Section D, 5.

———. "Mrs. Zaneis Favors County School Unit." November 9, 1935, 1.

———. "Mrs. Zaneis in Line for Post." July 3, 1937, 2.

———. "Mrs. Zaneis' Services Set." September 11, 1973, 54.

———. "Mrs. Zaneis Is Slated to Go." May 22, 1937, 1.

———. "Safety Work Opens Today." September 1, 1937, 2.

———. "State Board Ousts Durant School Chief." November 23, 1937, 1.

———. "State Board to Meet for Action on Aid." May 11, 1935, 2.

———. "Woman President at Durant Is Busy Living at Her Job." November 18, 1935, Section A, 4.

McGalliard, Mac. "Mrs. Zaneis Was a Fighter." *Daily Ardmoreite.* March 11, 1973, Section A, 54.

Milligan, James C. and Norris, L. David. "The First Lady of Education: Oklahoman Kate Galt Zaneis." *Chronicles of Oklahoma* 71 (1993) 276.

Way, Desda. "Kate Galt Zaneis." Federal Writers project, Biographical Sketches, Oklahoma Historical Society, Oklahoma City.

INDEX

ABOUT THE AUTHOR

Deborah Bouziden began writing and publishing magazine articles in 1985. She has published hundreds of articles, which have appeared in magazines such as *Writer's Digest, Woman's Day, The Writer, Personal Journaling, Byline, Lady's Circle, ParentLife, OKC Business,* and many others.

Bouziden has spoken and held writing workshops throughout the southwest for the Taos Institute of Art, Southwest Writers, National Association of Women Writers, Oklahoma Writers' Federation, and others. She has written and collaborated on numerous books, and is the author of *Oklahoma Off the Beaten Path, Insiders' Guide to Oklahoma City,* and *How to Start a Home-based House Painting Business* (Globe Pequot Press). Visit her at deborahbouziden.com

THE FOLLOWING CHAPTER IS EXCERPTED FROM:

MORE THAN PETTICOATS

Remarkable

KANSAS WOMEN

(January 2012, Paperback, $14.95, 978-0-7627-6027-5)

LILLA DAY MONROE

(1858–1929)

SUFFRAGIST AND JOURNALIST, COUNTING WOMEN'S VOTES AND STORIES

When she crept up to her grandmother's attic, Joanna Stratton didn't expect to find anything unusual. It was winter of 1975, and she was visiting her grandmother in Kansas while on break from Harvard. In all probability, she was bored.

Time moves slowly in the Midwest, especially when it's bitterly cold outside. When the air outside gets so cold it practically burns the skin to the touch, the whole world—for comfort's sake—shrinks down to the size of your home, where you can sit by the fire or burrow under a blanket with a cup of hot cocoa. So, with her world shrunk down to the size of an old Victorian home, Joanna went exploring upstairs.

It was something she always did when visiting her grandmother, this snooping around among tattered old ball gowns and once-fashionable hats, scanning titles of tattered books and magazines on dusty shelves, thumbing through boxes of family letters and silvery black-and-white photographs, opening trunks and drawers and cabinets to see what awaited her there. This was a day like any other day that Joanna had spent with relatives in Kansas.

Surely she must have known that her great-grandmother, the one who built this house in 1887, was a person of note in Kansas history. No doubt the family was proud that Lilla Day Monroe had been the first woman to practice law before the Kansas Supreme Court, that she had been a real spitfire and lobbied to have a statue dedicated to the memory of hardy pioneer women on the grounds of the Kansas State Capitol. The statue, still standing to this day, depicts a cloaked woman kneeling with an infant in one arm, the other arm wrapped around a studying boy, and a rifle slung across her knee. Her clothing drapes over her in a way that almost deifies her. This statue, Joanna must have known, was her grandmother's idea.

But she didn't go snooping through the attic looking for history with a capital *H*. She was just exploring, as we all do in grandparents' attics and basements, searching for clues about who our grandparents were before they were grandparents, who our parents were before they were parents, and, if we're lucky and our families have stayed in one place for long enough as Joanna's had, maybe even who our great-grandparents were before they were anything at all.

While indulging in this habitual time travel on that particular winter day, however, the dark-haired scholar stumbled upon the kind of thing scholars always dream of stumbling upon. She opened an old filing cabinet that had been pushed into a corner. Ducking her head to squeeze into the tight space, she began skimming the yellowing papers inside. She had just found the personal stories of eight hundred Kansas pioneer

Lilla Day Monroe Kansas Historical Society

women, written in their own words. In her introductory remarks for *Pioneer Women: Voices from the Kansas Frontier,* Stratton wrote:

> *It was an exhilarating moment of discovery for me. As I sat poring over the carefully penned writings, a human pageantry came alive for me. . . . I shivered with Emma Brown in her rain-soaked soddy. I watched Hannah Hoisington defend a neighbor's cabin against a pack of wolves and marveled as Jenny Marcy confronted a stampede of Texas longhorns. I celebrated Christmas day with little Harriet Adams and joined in a polka with lighthearted Catherine Cavender. I saw Anna Morgan held hostage by the Cheyenne. I witnessed Mrs. Lecleve endure childbirth alone in her cabin. I sang hymns with Lydia Murphy Toothaker and campaigned for woman suffrage with the Reverend Olympia Brown.*

Lilla Day Monroe had believed, correctly, that one day, people would care to know how these hardy women lived and endured in the state's earliest days. The cowboy and the railroad worker and the bootlegger and the soldier had all been hallowed and mythologized. Nobody had asked, just yet, what women had been up to all that time. But she knew, or maybe just hoped, that one day surely someone would. She suspected, however, that it might be too late to get answers, so she took it upon herself to ask the questions and to preserve the answers so that when people got around to asking, these eight hundred answers would exist.

She placed her original call for Kansas pioneer women's personal memoirs in a magazine she edited. Her intent was simply to run the responses in that very magazine's pages. She did publish a few of the stories that way, but quickly realized that the flood of responses merited more than a series of magazine stories, which ran the risk of being printed today and forgotten tomorrow. She decided to continue compiling stories and then to dedicate herself to organizing the material for an eventual book. She quit her substantial work outside the home to focus her efforts on this project full-time. Her mail was never boring. It contained heartache and triumph, suffering and redemption, once-ordinary details of a kind of daily life nearly forgotten by the early twentieth century. But Lilla got sick, and in 1929, she died before this grand opus ever saw print. Her great-granddaughter, Joanna Stratton, would complete and publish that book sixty-one years later, inspired by that fateful day spent rummaging in Lilla's attic.

Lilla Day Monroe was born in Indiana in 1858 and came to Kansas in 1884—at the tail end of what is now known as the "frontier era." She settled in Wakeeney, a western Kansas settlement created by pioneers traveling westward in search of better lives for themselves and their families. Many of them stopped about where Lilla stopped, at the midpoint between Kansas City and Denver, Colorado.

In short order, she met, fell in love, and married Lee Monroe, an attorney. Not only did she keep home and raise four children; she also clerked in her husband's law office. At home, she spent many grueling years stealing moments for her own study of the law. Eventually, she passed the bar exam. In 1895, Lilla Day Monroe became the first woman to practice before the Kansas Supreme Court. Knowing the law and the Constitution was important to her as she tirelessly championed what she believed to be the great causes of women—in particular, the cause of suffrage.

Her interest in the rights of women was sparked by a fairly ordinary scene that left a strong impression on her when she was just a little girl. On a visit to the general store, she happened to witness a disturbing scene.

A couple stood near the counter, and the woman asked the man if she could have a dollar. "To buy what?" the man asked. The woman explained that she needed a few things: some gingham, an apron. The other shoppers, like Lilla, could not help but eavesdrop. They became curious as to whether the woman would be given the dollar. Apparently, they did not do a very good job of pretending not to listen. The man realized he had an audience and played to it. Holding out the dollar, he quickly yanked it away as soon as his wife reached for it. When she realized she was being held up for ridicule, the woman began to cry—and so did Lilla. She would remember this story for the rest of her life.

In September 1906, she gave a talk on the history of the woman suffrage movement. In Kansas, at this time, women had the right to vote in municipal elections. This right had been granted decades earlier. And yet Kansas had not yet given its women the right to vote above and beyond the municipal level, and the United States had not yet granted universal suffrage.

Lilla began her speech frankly. "Before entering upon this history, I think it is my right to establish some sort of comradeship between myself and the gentlemen present by telling them just how it happens that I was chosen to make them miserable."

She went on. "No woman wants to talk on woman suffrage to a man. It is inevitable that the man should feel aggrieved. . . . You will go away feeling that I have said unpleasant things, and my committee that handed me the topic will not be able to help me bear the burden of your displeasure."

Lilla proceeded to relieve the men in her audience of any guilt the subject of woman suffrage might have caused them to feel, explaining that it was she and her sisters in arms whose responsibility it was to demand change. "[These] conditions are, have been, and will continue so long as women do not object."

And object Lilla did. She claimed that the vote was like the dollar that the woman in the general store had requested. She believed that women were being ridiculed for asking for something to which they had a basic, absolute right, and that for unfair reasons, only men could grant it. She argued that economic power and the right to vote were intertwined—that so long as women couldn't vote, politicians did not have much motivation to defend them. And she argued that the right to vote in municipal elections was only a few cents of the full dollar requested.

She fought for women's causes, not only as a lawyer and a speaker, but also as a journalist. She started and edited two magazines: *The Club Women* and *The Kansas Women's Journal*. And it was for these magazines that she began her project of recording and saving the stories of other pioneer women.

Teachers described the conditions trying to educate youth in a territory where school districts and formal public education systems had not yet been established, and where—for a time—schoolhouses had not been built. Textbooks could not be easily or cheaply shipped to rural areas, and teachers relied on whatever books the children were able to gather from their homes—often just tattered Bibles. Some taught in dugouts with dirt floors and walls, burlap hanging between the students and the walls so that the children would not go home covered in dirt. The students sat on benches. The teacher had no chalkboard.

Others taught in spare rooms of their own homes, or in students' houses; at the time, it was not unusual for teachers to live with students for a time, teach lessons, and then move on to the next home in the village. The funds did not exist to pay them well enough to secure their own lodgings, so this approach solved two problems at once. Teachers seemed to start working at around age sixteen or seventeen, and most were women simply because so few other opportunities were open to them. One teacher who submitted her memoirs boldly asserted that one-third of the women in Kansas at some point taught school. If the women included in this book are in any way representative, she was lowballing her estimate.

Lilla collected stories from farm wives confessing loneliness and isolation, and women who as young girls had helped their fathers out in the fields as well as their mothers inside the homes. She heard from a woman who had grown up in Abilene, where cattle stampeded as the guard dog lay snoring and her mother fainted from terror, leaving the girl to her own devices as she did her very best to wrangle the thousand or so bovines alone. There were women who hid from border ruffians during the Civil War years, and one whose mother went about town with a gun demanding that the pro-slavery man who wanted to kill her husband show himself so she could give him a piece of her mind, and maybe more.

Lilla's greatest accomplishment, perhaps, was to know how brave and strong the other women were in her midst, and to think their bravery and strength mattered enough that history might want to take note.

All eight hundred manuscripts she collected and organized were later typed by her daughter. After her great-granddaughter Joanna finished writing the book Lilla had been preparing to write herself, the complete collection of stories was donated to the Kansas State Historical Society, where students of history can still enjoy reading them today.